CHALLENGE OF THE ANDES

CHALLENGE
OF THE ANDES

The Conquest of Mount Huantsán

by

C. G. EGELER

in co-operation with

T. DE BOOY

translated from the Dutch by

W. E. JAMES

New York

DAVID McKAY COMPANY, INC.

CONTENTS

7

FOREWORD

I had the pleasure of meeting De Booy and Egeler in Amsterdam and heard from them something of their exciting story of climbing in the Andes.

Although the Andes are perhaps not as well known as the Himalayas, many of the problems met there are the same—the difficulties of establishing high camps; the sudden storms and the harsh cold; the dreadful weakness in the thin oxygen-starved air; and the sheer technical difficulties of ice and snow. It is an area that holds a strong fascination for the mountaineer with its numerous lofty unclimbed summits and its relative ease of access.

In their description of the first ascent of Huantsán, Egeler and De Booy cheerfully tell a story of a remarkable effort. To overcome such defences at such a height was an outstanding feat.

Perhaps my most vivid impression of meeting these men and reading their account is how they seemed to retain their sense of humour under every type of condition—sunshine or blizzard, gasping heat or bitter cold. Despite it all they battled on to the summit.

E. P. HILLARY

Auckland,
8th October 1954

9

ILLUSTRATIONS

ILLUSTRATIONS

FIGURES IN THE TEXT

IN ANTICIPATION

The events leading up to the Andes Expedition 1952 seem to me to be inextricably bound up with my own development. It had always been a youthful dream of mine to take part, if only once in my lifetime, in an expedition to some high mountain range outside Europe. This ambition was sparked in my case by a little incident, quite trivial in itself. I was a youngster of about ten when there came to dine with my parents a Dr. P. C. Visser, the leader of various Dutch expeditions, notably that to the Karakoram. He was lecturing that evening in Amsterdam and at table was telling of his climbing adventures in central Asia. I listened in fascination, so obviously enthralled that, after dinner, he suddenly invited me to help him sort out his lantern slides. While doing this, a new world opened before my eyes. All at once the towering peaks of the Himalayas became thrilling realities. The sight of snow-clad glaciers and precipitous heights aroused the strangest feelings in me; and then, in a flash, I knew—this is what I am going to do when I grow up, I told myself. I, too, will visit foreign mountain ranges.

Actually, even before this, I had acquired a love of mountaineering from my parents. When I was only four years of age they took me to the Swiss Alps. At first our visits were confined to the valleys, but soon I went with them on trips up the mountains. As I myself steadily grew, and as the climbs steadily increased in height and difficulty, so did I find myself becoming more and more a mountaineering devotee. The virus of Alpinism got into my blood. Indeed, it became so strong that I deliberately gave up my engineer-

13

ing studies at Delft in favour of a profession that involved contact with elemental Nature, with research at high altitude, i.e. Geology.

Most men feel the necessity of having something or other against which they can pit themselves. I have often wondered why, in my own case, this battling should be with mountains: why I should set such store on struggling against the icy elements with all their inherent dangers. Was it perhaps that in honourable contest with mountains and nature I found some compensation for the disappointments of ordinary day-to-day life? I don't know. But I confess that I get a sensation of glorious freedom and uplift when I am on glacier or on a lofty *arête*. But for the life of me, I cannot easily explain why.

Figuratively speaking, mountains large and small loom up in all our paths of life. Often their acute points can be evaded by deft side-stepping, by making—so to speak—a mental traverse along the face, or even sometimes by beating a discretionary retreat. But in real mountaineering things are different. There, the goal is definitely the summit; there can be no shirking the issue. The risks of the game are accepted. One weighs up beforehand what perils can fairly be faced; then follows the big assault. Retreat is out of the question unless of course the hazards make progress absolutely impossible. For me personally the most important thing was to know that I was prepared to devote myself wholeheartedly to the task of ascent. That alone contained real satisfaction. In time, even the eventual result of the climb took second place to the thrills of the assault.

Why go up mountains? Well—why any urge? Why does the artist paint? Why do men venture over the ocean in frail boats? Is it not perhaps that in casting adrift, one sometimes finds one's true self?

During the Second World War my usual summers in the mountains were interrupted; and after the war all sorts of circumstances made it impossible for me to get to the Alps. My youthful dream

did not seem to have the remotest chance of realization. 'The best years of my life' had already sped by. Participating in some expedition to some far-off range outside Europe was just a mirage—and would remain a mirage. Worse still, I seemed dispiritedly to have become quite reconciled to the situation, even reaching the stage of brusquely pushing aside reports of such expeditions, for their reminders of my youthful ambitions were too painful.

Then in the spring of 1949 something happened to jerk me out of this lethargy. Plans were announced of a Dutch expedition to the Himalayas under the leadership of a geologist, Dr. Klompé. What is more, applications to take part were invited from mountaineers and geologists. Needless to say, I could not resist the call. After much correspondence between Holland and Indonesia, where Prof. Klompé lived, I was accepted as a member. So was T. de Booy, another Amsterdam geologist with the same aspirations as myself.

Unfortunately, for various reasons—chiefly financial—this Himalayan project fell through. Nevertheless, although the expedition did not materialize, Prof. Klompé's initiative had other far-reaching repercussions, both for De Booy and myself. My eyes had been opened. How wrong it was to assume that my youthful dream could never come true!

Before this, however, De Booy and I had gone off to the French Alps at Chamonix, bent on improving our climbing skill and eager to acquire snow and ice techniques. Satisfactory results became quickly evident. We found it a pleasure to work together. We longed for further opportunities of teaming up. Whilst therefore these first trials in the Mont Blanc area were a direct consequence of Prof. Klompé's action the setting up later of our own Andes expedition was an indirect consequence. Only when we learned, in late 1950, that the Himalayan project was definitely off, did De Booy and I start looking round for something to take its place.

The idea of an expedition combining geological research and mountaineering had particular appeal for us, provided always that

the geological side remained the primary aim. We did not wish to separate the climbing from the surveying, but rather to blend the two. Such a combination, too, would make for economy—for about this one item we had no delusions whatsoever. Unless costs could be kept to an absolute minimum there was no chance of any Dutch expedition ever getting under way. This financial factor naturally ruled out mountains in Central Asia as a possible choice.

Where then? The answer was not too difficult. Running down the west side of South America are splendid mountain ranges. All the long way from the Caribbean Sea right down to Tierra del Fuego stretch the Andes in an interlocking series of mountain chains and mighty plateaux. Little or nothing is known about their geological structure. In many places magnificent unmastered peaks simply challenge a climber. Unlike the central Asian mountains, where expensive weeks of marching are needed to get even to the foothills, the Andes generally afford a quick approach.

That being so, the next point to decide was, which part of the Andes would best serve our purpose, bearing in mind two very important requirements: firstly, the ideal region should be one which, while remaining pretty well untapped from a research angle, would nevertheless offer good prospects of yielding interesting scientific results; secondly, the ideal region should contain some fairly high and, as yet, unclimbed peaks.

Here again the answer was simple. We turned immediately to the Cordillera Blanca, the highest range in the Peruvian Andes. It appeared the ideal mountain region for our purpose, for it was little known geologically, offered unique climbing possibilities, and was only a few days' march from Lima. Moreover, there existed a particularly fine topographical map of it, scaled 1 : 100,000, a precious gift to geologists.

Study of all the available relevant literature revealed that the southern portion of the range was least known from a geological aspect. There were other reasons, too—which need not be detailed

here[1]—why this part of the 'White Cordillera' offered us the maximum scope for certain specific studies. So, taking things by and large, we decided to map out a definite area in the southern part of the Cordillera Blanca. The precise limits of the zone could, of course, be varied if necessary, once we were out there.

Geological factors were thus decisive in influencing our choice, but we did not neglect the mountaineering possibilities. In the northern portion of our designated area there were several peaks rising to 20,000 feet and over. All had already been climbed, with the exception of the Huantsán, which rose to nearly 21,000 feet and was at that time the loftiest unconquered peak in the entire chain, and, indeed, in whole Peru. In Kinzl and Schneider's excellent book entitled the *Cordillera Blanca, Perú*, Kinzl wrote: 'Farther to the south is the Nevado Huantsán (20,981 feet), not only the highest peak, but at the same time the uncontested monarch, reigning supreme over the entire southern half of the Cordillera Blanca. All other peaks look unimportant beside it, especially if viewed from the east.'

The ascent of this mighty Huantsán was the chief mountaineering goal of our expedition. Little was actually said about it at first, because descriptions of the peak made it seem too formidable to attempt. How could such a dread fortress of snow and ice succumb to such a small and-partly-comparatively inexperienced band of climbers? We talked instead about two smaller, more southerly mountains; the Caullaraju and the Pongos, thinking that it would perhaps be better to attempt one of these before looking elsewhere. Before leaving the Netherlands, however, we heard that the Caullaraju had been climbed by an Italian group. So we were left with the Pongos massif as our first objective.

As it happened, our expedition succeeded in climbing the Nevado Queshque in this massif; and also the highest top in the entire group, the Nevado Pongos itself. Emboldened by these two victories, we

[1] See chapter on Geology.

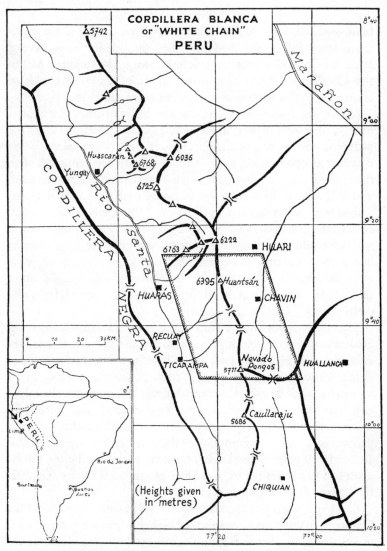

Map showing the Cordillera Blanca and the expeditionary area.

started the assault on the Huantsán. Twice the mountain foiled our attacks; then finally it yielded. These three ascents were the rich harvest of our mountaineering efforts. The Cordillera Blanca certainly proved ideal for a small group of climbers and the geological explorations in the chain yielded results as gratifying to us as our climbing successes.

A youthful dream had come true.

THE TEAM

Once the area to be explored had been broadly fixed, the next step was to decide how many members our expedition should have. The surveying side was simple: De Booy and I thought we could manage that part quite well between us. The saying 'Two's company, three's none' applies very aptly to field-work in difficult terrain. A third man in such a case is often an unproductive unit.

But on the mountaineering side, a party of only two would be quite insufficient. It was essential to get another mountaineer, if not two, to join us. What is more, to have a reasonable chance of securing our objectives, one of our companions would definitely have to be a highly skilled Alpinist. This, as it happened, turned out to be Lionel Terray, a professional guide from Chamonix. Force of circumstances rendered it impossible for us to get a fourth man.

We first met Terray by pure chance. When De Booy and I went to the French Alps in the summer of 1950 we needed the services of a guide for a few weeks to accompany us on some of the classic climbs in the Mont Blanc area. In front of the 'Bureau des Guides' at Chamonix we encountered a pleasant-looking young fellow wearing the guide's badge, to whom we explained exactly what we had in mind. Somehow or other he did not appear so enthusiastic as we would have liked. With the excuse that he was not free for some days, he whisked us over to another guide with the remark:

'Ah, Lionel, these seem *just* the clients for you!' We learned later
that the real reason for his not taking us on was not that he was
engaged, but that he preferred earning money a little less strenu-
ously.

So willy-nilly, and rather dubiously, we came in contact with this
other unknown guide, who looked in fact, much too youthful for
the tough exercising we had in mind. Imagine then our surprise to
learn that it was none other than Lionel Terray—a guide whose
name was then on everybody's lips in Chamonix. That spring he
had taken part in a French Himalayan expedition which had been
the first ever to get up to 26,247 feet (8,000 m.) and to scale the
Annapurna. A better man could not have been found for tutoring
us in snow and ice.

Terray had won early laurels for his many accomplished climbs
in the Alps, notably the second ascent of the notorious north wall
of the Eiger in the Bernese Oberland. Before joining us in the Cordillera Blanca, he took part in the French Patagonian expedition
which, in the winter of 1951-2, succeeded in mastering the terrible
Fitz Roy on the Argentine-Chilian border. Terray is undeniably
one of the greatest living masters of his craft. His mountaineering
record puts him in a class of his own.

Chance brought us all together that summer. Shortly after that
first meeting we made various difficult climbs on ice and rock, and
a close bond of friendship developed between us. It led all three of
us eventually to the snow-capped giants in the Cordillera Blanca.
Out in Peru, when we recalled that first meeting, Terray was always
tickled to hear how we had taken him at first sight for a callow
youngster.

Actually, it had not been Terray we originally had in mind for
heading the mountaineering side of our Andes expedition. We had
already approached the famous Swiss Alpinist, André Roch, whom
I had previously met on one or two occasions. He was not only a
guide of international repute, but a man of science. His long service

20

with the Swiss Snow and Avalanche Research Institute had given him a rich experience, particularly on glacial terrain. This, and his many expeditions to mountain ranges outside Europe, made him the ideal leader of our undertaking. But Fate willed otherwise. In the autumn of 1951 plans were afoot for a Swiss expedition to Mount Everest, and Roch, who had already been on several occasions to the Himalayas, was naturally chosen. To take part in an expedition attacking the greatest mountain in the world is, of course, the highest ambition of every mountaineer. Although Roch chivalrously regarded himself as under obligation to us, we naturally gave him complete freedom of choice in the circumstances.

Meanwhile, during our mountaineering trips with Terray, we gathered that he regretted not having met us before we had contacted Roch. So when Roch finally fell out, all our hopes were immediately pinned on Terray. We were lucky. Just as we were about to get in touch, a letter from him arrived. He, too, had heard of Roch's new plans and offered to step into the breach, his only stipulation being that we should decide quickly as he was leaving within a week for South America with the French Patagonian expedition. Needless to say, we gratefully grasped the offer. De Booy set off the same night to Paris to settle matters and to discuss all sorts of issues concerning provisions and equipment. The next day the whole thing was tied up; and so it was that though a Swiss of international repute had dropped out, within forty-eight hours a Frenchman of international repute had come in with us.

Terray and De Booy had talked of the desirability of getting a fourth to join the expedition. Terray agreed to sound a friend of his, Raymond Grière, a commercial attaché at the French legation in Bogotá. Grière was an accomplished climber and, as he already resided in Colombia, his participation would involve us in less travel costs.

Grière, himself, impressed us as most enthusiastic when he came to Amsterdam some months later during a spell of leave in Europe.

Then came an unfortunate setback. Whilst training on the cliffs near Fountainebleau, Grière was the victim of an unlucky fall, resulting in a dislocated arm. So, before the expedition had even started, our fourth man was out.

When our intentions became known in Holland we were inundated with offers from young men wanting to come with us. There were ex-service men, just returned from Indonesia, who seemingly could not adjust themselves to everyday life. Others saw in this a cheap way of sneaking as emigrants into America. Then there were the venturing type, like a couple who recommended themselves as —not geologists, but a pair of lusty Dutch youngsters, full of grit and 'Holland's Glory'. Most had not much to offer. One aspirant quoted a past reeking with lurid adventure. He made such a song of his many-sided abilities that we ourselves almost became convinced that there was no chance of success without him. In 1951 he had gone big-game hunting in Tanganyika and had made a study of wild life, his speciality being snakes. Among many remarkable characteristics were his heavily-muscled physique which had never known sickness, his dexterity in handling canoes in rapids, his intimate knowledge of many native races and his human interest in the coloured 'man in the street'. He was an artist with the camera, expert in preparing reports, ski-ing, horse-riding, swimming, sailing, long-distance running, and in addition to his exceptional powers of endurance he had a fair knowledge of basic Spanish, practical experience of climbing—and endless other merits.

We were, alas, obliged to disappoint all these enthusiasts. What we needed were experienced mountaineers. But this did not mean that we did not esteem these offers.

PREPARATIONS

It is extraordinarily difficult to give a just description of the vast amount of preparatory work involved in launching our moun-

taineering expedition. There were so many sides to it. Our own physical and technical training was, of course, of the highest importance. De Booy and I began in the summer of 1950—it was then with a view to our participating in the proposed Dutch expedition to the Himalayas. We went to Chamonix for a month to exercise on peaks in the Mount Blanc massif. Besides improving our technique, we wanted to get to know each other's powers; and, of course, weaknesses, so as to obviate any later awkward surprises. With Terray we made numbers of climbs on snow and ice, and also on rock. He imparted secrets of icemanship, in which craft there were few who could equal his virtuosity. His patience with us was infinite, although generally he was not the long-suffering type of teacher. For hours on end he chaperoned us up the Glacier des Bossons, scaling the most unprepossessing ice-walls and teaching us how to use crampons to tackle a slope of 60 degrees without cutting a single step with the axe.

On our first big ice-trip he led us to the steep north face of the Aiguille de Chardonnet. It was an audacious project that nearly brought disaster. Owing to my lack of technique I had a nasty fall whilst negotiating a tricky passage not far from the top. Terray had difficulty in holding me on the rope, but all I heard afterwards was his laconic: 'Ah, vous êtes lourd, Kees!'

After eleven years of rustication those first training trips were not too easy for me. It was a case of starting anew, but with the added disadvantages of increased weight and less muscular flexibility.

Sometimes it seemed difficult for Terray to realize that everyone was not so expert as himself. This led on one occasion to hard words. There was I, precariously stuck on a smooth precipitous rock face, feeling absolutely at the end of my tether and vainly trying to seek higher holds, when I heard his buoyant: 'Ah, Kees, c'est facile ici. . . . Il y a des prises partout!' It was too annoying and frustrating for words.

But the important thing was that we certainly did learn a lot in

that strenuous summer of 1950. And our physical training continued relentlessly during the winter months, too. De Booy and I went on every possible occasion to the south of Dinant, where the steep cliffs along the Meuse proved ideal for improving technique and keeping tendons supple.

In the summer of 1951 we were again at Chamonix, working through an extensive programme of climbs, although illness unfortunately prevented me from participating in the most important part of this training. De Booy appreciably improved his snow and ice techniques and reached the stage of being able to make some truly wonderful guide-less climbs.

The following winter saw us so preoccupied with the many details connected with our impending departure to South America that we had little or no opportunity for training in the Ardennes. We kept ourselves fit by running and indoor training. De Booy had been doing this for years. Regularly every morning he used to run full tilt up a hill, known locally as the Aerdenhoutse Kopje.

It was somewhat more difficult for me in Amsterdam. I had to content myself with sprinting through the flat Vondel park, where the many ponds did at least enable me to vary my route from time to time. Day in and day out, eventually with increasing ease, I could be seen all through the winter of 1951-2 pounding round the ponds —often the object of derisive hoots from early morning visitors to the park. In the beginning it was quite a job for me to ignore these rude bawlers and resist the temptation to stop and shout back. After a while they all got used to seeing me. It was only occasionally that I heard a bantering shout: 'Hi, no need to chase like that— they've already caught that thief!' This running was the part of my training I liked least, but it was well worth while. It is no exaggeration to say that it doubled my staying powers. I strongly recommend anyone planning summer ascents to do the same.

Physical training was, of course, only one phase of our preparations. There was a frightful lot to do in other directions. It was im-

perative, for instance, to put the undertaking on a sound financial footing. Correspondence relating to possible grants from scientific and cultural bodies increased from day to day, and the discussions necessarily involved thereby took up a great deal of precious time.

It was necessary, too, to visit all the firms from which we were getting provisions and equipment in order to discuss with experts on the spot the most suitable types, precise quantities, and the best sorts of packing for all our stores. De Booy fortunately had more time at his disposal than I, and for four whole months prior to our departure he was hard at it from morning to night, coping with all the details of food, material and gear. How excellently he functioned in this respect was apparent later on during the expedition itself; we literally wanted for nothing.

A problem of particular moment to us was the matter of insurance against accident. It was perhaps not altogether surprising that most of the big companies appeared singularly uninterested in our particular type of risk. Luckily, just before our departure, one insurance firm did meet us and accepted our liability on reasonable terms.

Everything eventually sorted itself out. The interest and cooperation we received from a variety of sources exceeded all our expectations and contributed in no small measure to the success of our enterprise.

TO THE ANDES

De Booy, Terray, and I travelled separately and by different routes to South America. De Booy was the first to set off on the big journey. He left on April 5th by the s.s. *Baarn* belonging to the Royal Dutch Steamship Company. The ship was calling at many ports and it was four weeks before she reached Callao, the Peruvian port near Lima.

I followed on April 24th but as I travelled by K.L.M.-Dutch

Airlines, via Curaçao and Venezuela, I arrived in Peru before De Booy. Terray intended to leave early in June by K.L.M. Airlines, taking the southern route.

On April 30th there I was, standing on the quayside at Callao as the s.s. *Baarn* emerged through the early morning sea-mist and steamed into the harbour. Although I had already been away a week, it was only then that I felt the thrill of belonging to an expedition. On board with De Booy was all the expeditionary equipment, seventy-six cases weighing nearly two tons. Once these were unloaded we would be able to make a real start. As the ship was somewhat overdue I had to wait several hours on the quayside. Whilst sauntering about, I was repeatedly buttonholed by dark-hued youngsters offering their services as porters. I had not been long enough in South America to acquire anything but the scantiest knowledge of Spanish, so my exchanges, particularly with one persistent boy, were reduced to gestures. As the ship neared the quay De Booy's first sight of me was in gesticulating debate with a half-breed—a spectacle which was soon to become commonplace.

I was glad to tell him, on greeting, that following approaches by our ambassador, the Peruvian Government had agreed to waive all duties on our stores and gear. In our simplicity we thought that this meant we could cart off everything as soon as it was unloaded, without having to undergo any of the usual Customs formalities. How mistaken we were! We were asked to call at the Custom House during the afternoon—just to regularize this and that. Actually we didn't mind this a bit, for it happened to be the birthday of our gracious Queen Juliana, and in honour of the occasion there was to be a reception at noon in the Dutch Embassy. So to De Booy's joyous surprise, and within two hours of his arrival in Peru, there he was quaffing champagne! A lively start indeed to what turned out to be an indescribably hectic week, for we had to attend to a multiplicity of matters in Lima and visit dozens and dozens of people.

26

The Customs' business did not prove at all so straightforward as we had fondly imagined. True enough, when we entered the shed that afternoon our seventy-six cases were all nicely piled up, but taking them away appeared to be quite another matter. There was a grim succession of forms to be filled in and signed. In Holland we had religiously listed the contents of each crate, case, and bag, declaring every single item down to the last detail. The lists were all in French. Now a polite Customs officer informed us that every individual item must be translated into Spanish.

Realizing with sick dismay that this would take days, De Booy and I mustered up our best Spanish. This unreasonable request would throw our carefully timed programme entirely out of gear. It was quite impossible for us to find the precise equivalent Spanish terms for our geological instruments and extensive medical outfit. We made a poignant appeal to them to spare us this great calamity.

After a lot of talk and hurried consultations, we gathered with relief that we had gained this point. But that didn't mean we were yet in the clear. Further delay was caused by the fact that May 1st was a national holiday in Perú and all public services were closed. We ourselves were fully occupied the day after that with engagements, but eight o'clock on Saturday morning found us again in the Customs shed. This time some headway was made, and we were given to understand that we could come on Monday morning and fetch everything away. Tidings of good cheer indeed! On Monday we would be away from Lima and able to start the expedition proper!

On Sunday we took the opportunity to see a bullfight. It was an unforgettable spectacle. We enjoyed the colour, the atmosphere, the terrific enthusiasm of the onlookers.

Up to then we had given ourselves no time at all to get any close impression of South-American life, but in the near future we hoped to get better acquainted. We particularly wanted to speed up our journey towards the Cordillera Blanca. Thanks to the good services

of Mr. Corver, the Royal Dutch Steamship Company's inspector, we were able to hire a Ford lorry. Punctually at eight on Monday morning we drove it into the Customs shed, but—once again we had been too optimistic. There was another hitch. We were asked to sign a declaration that everything we were importing would in due course be exported. It was a sheer impossibility. More than half of our cases contained special tinned foods which we should eat at high altitudes. Now we *were* at our wits' end. This time it looked as though we had definitely reached a deadlock. Just as we were giving up hope of getting away that day a saviour appeared in the guise of one of the steamship agents. The genial Charlie swept in to our aid and soon found a formula which satisfied the demands of all concerned. Guarantees were given, and everything was settled. The Customs staff were the first to congratulate us on the final happy result.

To the accompaniment of much affability we loaded our cases. All this had taken five hours. It was half-past one before we got away. De Booy and I intended to ride on the lorry, bearing in mind the age-old golden rule for travellers: 'Never part with your luggage.'

Our lorry driver looked a queer mixture of white, black, and Indian blood, but he certainly could handle the truck. At first we could not ride in the lorry as such vehicles are not allowed to carry passengers within the confines of Lima, so we hired a splendid Chevrolet station-wagon complete with radio and half-Indian chauffeur. In that we rode jubilantly out of Lima to the tune of Beethoven's Piano Concerto No. 1. On to the great adventure!

After passing a control post, about six miles out of the city, we took our places in the lorry. A long journey of well over 200 miles now lay before us. The lorry had to take us to the small village of Ticapampa in the Santa valley. It nestled at the foot of the Cordillera Blanca and was therefore close to our exploratory area. To get there we first had to cross the Cordillera Negra, a range rising to over 13,000 feet and bordering the Santa valley on the west.

For several hours we sped across a desert stretching along the coast. Near the village of Patavilca the road swung inland and almost immediately we started climbing towards the pass. In Lima they had told us some horrifying stories about this shockingly steep route up to the pass. Glancing at our chauffeur, we noticed him solemnly making the sign of the cross. De Booy would have it that this had something to do with the perils of the road ahead. Luckily for our peace of mind it soon became dark so that we could not look down into, and therefore remained blissfully unaware of, the dizzy depths at the winding roadside.

It took five hours to climb 13,000 feet from sea level to the pass. Mile after mile went by. The driver seemed tireless, but De Booy and I soon became drowsy. Perhaps it was the monotonous whine of the engine in low gear, or maybe the effects of the thin air to which we were not yet attuned. According to the driver, the lorry, too, suffered from altitude. Engine power was reduced by about 40 per cent owing to lack of oxygen.

It was past midnight when we reached the pass. We were fated, however, not to carry on much further. Hardly had we begun to run downhill than De Booy and I were jolted awake by a frightful noise and a nasty shock. Before the lorry had time to falter to a standstill I had jumped out, dragging De Booy with me. Everything was shrouded in thick smoke. Were we on fire? Was all the precious gear going up in flames? Luckily it wasn't so bad as that. The back axle had broken, and the rear double wheels on the right had come clean off. They now lay on the roadside some distance behind us. What I had taken for smoke turned out to be a smother of thick dust caused by the broken axle digging a long groove in the road. We stood there, sombrely looking at our damaged vehicle, by no means fully appreciating the peril in which we had been. Months later, on our return from the Cordillera Blanca to Lima, we passed that way in daylight and stared aghast at the sheer drop fringing the roadside. Had the accident occurred five minutes ear-

lier, whilst still climbing up, we should inevitably have hurtled down into the abyss. Our expedition would have calamitously ended before it had even begun.

Anyway, there we were, standing numbly in the road at midnight, over 13,000 feet up, with no hope of further progress. Our driver set us an example of decisive action in such circumstances. Briefly summing-up the situation, he climbed without further ado into the lorry and in a few minutes was asleep.

This was our signal to fetch our sleeping bags. There wasn't enough room for the three of us in the lorry cabin; in any case, it was not too fresh inside. So making the best of a bad job, we settled down at the roadside. We were already feeling the effects of the high altitude; it was as though we were a trifle tipsy. It was also icy cold. When we woke at dawn the tops of our sleeping bags were covered with hoarfrost, but the bags themselves had stood the test. We, ourselves, had not suffered in the slightest from cold in the night.

During the early morning numbers of lorries came by, some carrying whole gangs of Indians in the open parts at the back. This seemed to be the local method of transport. At last we managed to stop a lorry going in the direction we wanted and to secure a lift on it for De Booy. He was to get to Ticapampa and try to hire another lorry there, while I remained, keeping an eye on the baggage.

All day went by before he returned with a truck. During that time I succumbed to the 'Soroche', the notorious Andes type of mountain sickness. The transition from sea level to 13,000 feet or more had been too quick for my body to get acclimatized. I had a splitting headache and felt miserably sick and fit for nothing. When De Booy finally turned up I was too out of sorts to be of any help in transferring the gear. The only thought that cheered was the prospect now of getting down to a lower level, even if it were only some 2,000 feet.

Dismal though I felt, the breathtaking panorama which met our eyes during the descent towards the Santa valley held me spellbound. During the long climb the previous evening we had just caught a glimpse in the distance of the first few snowy caps of the Cordillera Blanca, silhouetted against the clear evening sky. Now, as we rode down, the whole mountain chain slowly but surely came into view to its full extent. In the north rose the mighty Huascarán, the highest mountain in the region. We recognized it immediately from the many photos we had seen. But it was not the only impressive sight. To the south stretched an almost continuous succession of ice giants, each vying with the others in steepness. But there was one towering above the rest, so formidable in appearance that it caught our particular attention. It was the Huantsán, our goal, our own *pièce de resistance*. This first sight of it was enough to make anyone fall a prey to forebodings. Did we really intend to battle with this mighty fortress? Were we not aiming a lot too high? This initial view certainly did nothing to bolster up my own morale. I suddenly felt exceedingly small and insignificant, and brooded over our rashness in daring even to consider an attempt at this imposing pyramid. Further south the chain developed into a number of separate massifs, amongst which was the Pongos. It was here that our first attempts would be made.

Arriving at last in Ticapampa, we made our way forthwith to the premises of the Anglo-French Ticapampa Silver Mining Company to pay our respects. The management had previously promised us all sorts of facilities, and we rather hoped that one or two sheds might be put at our disposal to house our baggage. Perhaps we ourselves might also be able to find accommodation here for our stay in the valley.

Our welcome exceeded our wildest expectations. We were immediately allocated a house for the whole duration of the expedition in which to store all our gear, and this wasn't all. We were warmly invited to consider ourselves the guests of Mr. Kroupnitzky, the

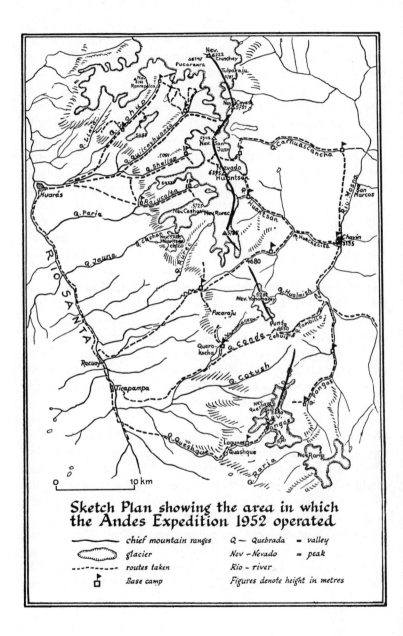

Sketch Plan showing the area in which the Andes Expedition 1952 operated

—— chief mountain ranges	Q — Quebrada	= valley
glacier	Nev – Nevado	= peak
------- routes taken	Rio ~ river	
Base camp	Figures denote height in metres	

mine manager, and his wife. Needless to say we grasped this kind offer, as the Dutch say, with both hands.

From then on Ticapampa, nestling in the shadow of the 'White Chain', became the headquarters of our expedition and was the point from which we sallied forth on all the geological and mountaineering trips we were to make in the next few months.

THE HISTORY OF 'ANDINISME' IN THE CORDILLERA BLANCA

The first sight of the enormous glaciers in the Cordillera Blanca renders it difficult for anyone to realize how close these mountains are to the Equator. The 'White Chain' is actually the highest tropical range in the world. The Himalayas are higher, but they lie outside the torrid zone. No less than twenty-nine peaks in the Cordillera Blanca rise to over 20,000 feet. In height, therefore, they greatly exceed the Alps, and although among these twenty-nine there may be a few which, technically speaking, are not so very difficult to climb, most of the others—because of their precipitousness, their often well-nigh vertical faces, and their razor-edged ridges—command the deep respect of every climber coming to Peru.

Over the years a range of such distinction as the Cordillera Blanca naturally attracted the attention of mountaineers from all over the world, for here were numbers of glittering peaks, still unconquered and conveniently situated in a region to which there was easy access.

At first it was the highest peak, the Huascarán, which mainly lured the mountaineers. The south summit, reaching 22,205 feet, caps all other peaks in the group; but, from a climber's point of view, the Huascarán is technically less difficult than some of its neighbours rising to 20,000 feet and over. Attempts were already

33

being made at the beginning of the century on the Huascarán. An Englishman, C. R. Enoch, visited the area in 1903 and was so impressed that he returned in 1904 to attack the giant from the west side. The attempt carried him about 17,000 feet. Then, beset by overwhelming difficulties, he was forced to withdraw.

Enoch was not the only one with designs on the Huascarán. In the same year, and again in 1906 and 1908, half a dozen assaults were made by a lady, Miss Annie Peck, an ambitious American journalist. In the last two attempts she was supported by two excellent Swiss guides, Taugwalder and Zumtaugwald. According to Miss Peck, the north summit, then regarded as the highest point, was actually reached during the last assault. But this attempt had tragic consequences, for the group were caught by a blizzard during the descent and marooned for several days at a high altitude. One of the guides suffered severely from frost-bitten hands and feet. Later amputations rendered him an invalid for the rest of his life.

The altimeter had been left behind in the valley, but Miss Peck estimated the height of the Huascarán as 24,000 feet. She thereupon claimed to have broken the world high-altitude climbing record for ladies, a coveted distinction previously held by a Mrs. Bullock-Workman for a high ascent in the Himalayas. The latter's reaction was as unexpected as extravagant. Dissatisfied with being relegated to second place, she equipped an expedition—said to have cost her at least 13,000 dollars—to ascertain the precise height of the Huascarán. In a certain sense, however, she had her money's worth, for the Huascarán proved to be by no means as high as Miss Peck had claimed (it was actually 22,205 feet instead of 24,000 feet), and furthermore the north summit, which Miss Peck had climbed, was not so high as the south summit. Indeed, her claim to have climbed the north summit was itself disputed. Declarations made by her fellow-climbers—whom she had left behind, ill and without means, in Perú—threw grave doubts, to say the least of it, on her claim. One thing was however certain. Miss Peck's group did reach the so-

called 'Garganta', a saddle between the north and south summits. That much was substantiated.

A sound basis for the geographical and alpinistic explorations of the Cordillera Blanca was laid by three expeditions sent by the Austro-German Alpine Club during the years 1932, 1936 and 1939. The members included a number of outstanding mountaineers. The first expedition scaled the higher south summit of the Huascarán. Thereafter the good work continued apace. Members of the expeditions made numerous first ascents, among them no less than fourteen mountains towering above the 20,000-ft. mark. Some of these were very tough propositions indeed.

Never before in mountaineering history has a range of such extent been so thoroughly scoured in so short a space of time. When one reads the reports of these climbs in Borcher's excellent book *Die Weisse Kordillere*, studies the text and photos in Kinzl and Schneider's outstanding *Cordillera Blanca (Perú)*, or peruses the annals of the sponsoring club, one cannot help admiring the magnificent work done by these intrepid men. The three expeditions did not merely indulge in record-breaking climbs. On the contrary! A tremendous amount of scientific research work was carried out. Among the many things for which we were grateful to these untiring pioneers was their preparation of a topographical map embracing the whole chain, scaled 1: 100,000. During our stay in the Cordillera Blanca we had ample proof of the excellent quality of this charting work.

During the Second World War exploration remained a dead letter in the area. The only climbing reported was by a group of North-American students, whose aim was the ascent of the Huarascán, still apparently the main attraction as the highest peak in the range. The assault seems to have fizzled out before any great height was reached.

Some years after the war there was a renewal of activity, starting with a Swiss Alpine group which, amongst other things, climbed two peaks of over 20,000 feet. Encouraged by this, they attempted

a third equally lofty peak, the Alpamayo, probably the loveliest in the Andes. But this fantastic ice pyramid proved nearly fatal to the Swiss climbers. A third of the way up, the whole group broke through a cornice, deceptively overhanging the ridge, and plunged some 1,000 feet into the depths. By miraculous good fortune, they all landed in soft snow.

Three years later, in the summer of 1951, the Alpamayo bowed its proud head to members of a Franco-Belgian expedition. After a gruelling ascent they achieved success where the Swiss had failed. Before this, however, a Franco-Belgian attack on the Huascarán had failed, possibly because the expedition had not given its members sufficient time to get acclimatized.

This, then, was the situation when De Booy and I began planning our own expedition to the southern part of the Cordillera Blanca. In the spring of 1952, prior to our departure, a group of Italian mountaineers visited this part of the chain and climbed the most southerly peak of any importance, the Caullaraju (18,654 feet).

We came into the field a few months later with our Franco-Dutch expedition. The story of our ascents forms the major part of this book. Following the climbing of several lesser peaks, the expedition was fortunate enough to succeed in making a first ascent of the Huantsán, which towered to a height of 20,981 feet and was, up to that time, the highest unconquered mountain in the whole 'White Chain'.

In the same period an American expedition, operating more to the north, climbed one of the peaks rising to over 20,000 feet in the Huandoy group.

With this, the history of Andinism in the Cordillera Blanca closes for the time being. The last word, however, is certainly not yet spoken. Although an imposing number of the highest peaks in the Cordillera Blanca have now been subdued, there still remain hosts of wonderful possibilities for the mountaineer. There still are numbers of summits towering to over 20,000 feet and as yet unchal-

lenged. Some, of course, are only secondary summits of mountains already climbed, but there are many others well worth an attempt. Among these last strongholds to repel the onslaught of mountain climbers towers the terrifying Chacraraju, which rearing up to 19,684 feet, is a fantastically steep ice giant and rightly regarded as the stiffest problem in the whole range. Some expedition or other will assuredly, in the not distant future, mark this down as an objective.

As to the other unconquered peaks—they include several very intriguing mountaineering 'subjects', even though these may not tower up to the 20,000-ft. level. As we ourselves found when tackling the Pongos, which was *only* 18,737 feet, some mountains, although smaller, may nevertheless present more than enough technical difficulties to command the sincere respect of attackers. We found the Pongos almost as difficult as the Huantsán itself.

Peaks like the Tulparaju (18,987 feet), the San Juán (19,170 feet), the Chico Huantsán (18,711-feet.) and the Chico Pongos (18,635 feet)—to name but a few—are worthy objects of the climber's attention. Then there is the 18,770 ft. high Nevado Cayesh, a razor-edged tower, compared with which none of the tops in the Cordillera Blanca, soaring though they may up to 20,000 feet, can compare in savage perpendicularity.

In this region, where so much ground lay fallow, it was natural for climbers to head for their objectives by the easiest possible routes. But once all the tops have succumbed, the time will come here, too, when stout hearts will be searching for paths up other seemingly impossible faces, in order to return home with some new achievement. The fascinating possibilities for mountaineers are indeed unlimited.

THE PONGOS MASSIF

AN UNNAMED MOUNTAIN

It had been our intention to start the mountain-climbing side of our expedition about June 1st. So once we had concluded our geological survey of a portion of the chain, De Booy and I returned on May 25th to Ticapampa to await Lionel Terray. Alas, a letter from him was lying there, saying that he had been obliged to postpone his journey by a whole week owing to the dislocation of air services caused by strikes in the American oil industry.

This was unfortunate. But we had now come to realize that all plans would have to be elastic, and we decided to put our time to some use as far as possible. We had intended, once Terray was with us, to set off immediately to the southern part of the chain and make an attempt on the Pongos, the highest peak in the southern massif. Terray or no Terray, we now decided to go there all the same and make a geological survey. Arrangements were made whereby Terray could come along later and join us at our base camp.

Up to now, we had taken only one native helper on our high-altitude surveying trips, his job being to release us as much as possible from time-devouring camp chores, and to act as bearer as and when required. The Silver Mine management had been good enough to allocate us one of their foremen, Blasido Bañes, for this purpose. As he had proved very useful in the past few weeks, we proposed to take him with us now.

The combination of surveying work with mountain climbing

would obviously require the help of more than one porter. To assist us in carrying loads from base to advanced camps we secured another man, named Eugenio, who had gone with us on a previous occasion as a mule-driver and had let us know that he enjoyed this sort of work. So, early on June 1st, with these two half-Indians, plus an *arriero*, or groom, and six pack animals, we made our way out of the Santa valley.

The distance from Ticapampa to the foot of the Pongos massif was covered comfortably in one day, despite delays caused by a few lazy donkeys in the string. We could thus appreciate to the full what decided advantage the short approach to the Cordillera Blanca afforded. Provided one's base point is selected with care, the foothills can be reached in a very short time. The little village of Ticapampa, in this respect, was ideally situated for our purpose.

The route led over the monotonous pampa, where the scenery was nothing much to write home about, and then into the long Queshque valley. Our thoughts were concentrated on our goal, the Pongos with its 18,737 feet of climbing. Lying to the extreme south, it was barely visible from Ticapampa, although it was the loftiest top in the southern massif. At first, some of the neighbouring peaks seemed distinctly higher, but as we came nearer, this proved an optical illusion.

Near a group of mountains on the north side of the Queshque valley, we saw at last one distinct peak rearing up on the south side. This was the Pongos, but somehow it did not seem so very impressive from where we were. In fact, De Booy burst out, 'I say, is that all? Well, if we can't get up there, we might as well give up climbing!'

Penetrating more deeply into the valley, we rounded a bend at about 14,000 feet and suddenly there towered the mountain in its full glory, dominating the valley almost as completely as the Matterhorn overshadows the Zermatt valley. From then on, all compla-

cency vanished. There was no more airy talk. We became all too conscious of the Pongos' sharp ridges and precipitous walls.

As dusk fell on June 1st, we pitched our base camp in full view of the peak. In the rays of the setting sun its snowy majestic dome looked superb. Wreaths of mist playing over the sharp ascending ridge made the mountain look ethereally beautiful.

At base camp we had a roomy tent 8 ft. × 13 ft. × 8 ft. with an extension running out another 6½ feet. Not only could we stand upright in this tent, but we could also eat at a table, for we had brought out with us a folding table and stools—a luxury we were more fully to appreciate when we came down from the higher assault camps. To house the bearers we had a two-man tent and a three-man tent, and in addition a small tent was provided for storing gear, provisions, etc.

Our first few days in the Queshque valley were devoted to a geological survey of the area. Although waiting for Terray, we did not want to waste our time. If we could map the massif now there would be no need to return later to complete our geological researches. Our explorations on the second day enabled us to make a reconnaissance along the base of the Pongos with a view to assessing the best side for an attack. We wandered up to the end of the Queshque valley, where a fairly large glacier ended. Ascending this glacier for several hours, we finally obtained a vantage point from which we had an excellent view of the entire west flank of the Pongos. It at once became clear that the mountain would have to be attacked via one of its sharp ridges. The face in front of us was definitely unassailable.

Our previous knowledge of the mountain had been more or less derived from a photograph in the book by Kinzl and Schneider. Taken from the south, it gave a good view of the south-west ridge, which looked fairly simple. We had accordingly regarded this as the most suitable route. But at closer quarters we could see some steep propositions high up which were not shewn at all in the

picture. Indeed, the variations between the photo and actuality were so great that we wondered whether this was the selfsame ridge! On looking again, however, we could pick out enough similarities to remove our doubts.

Later on, when Terray arrived in the Pongos area and was told about this, he ventured the opinion that a big landslide must have

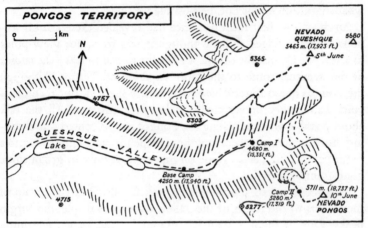

Sketch map of the Pongos massif.

taken place, resulting in the collapse of a considerable portion of the original face.

The south-west ridge had thus become appreciably more difficult than anticipated; but it certainly offered possibilities, although two formidable obstacles were obvious. For much of the way up, and poised over the edge of the ridge, was a massive cornice.[1] Our field-glasses also revealed a particularly steep and unpromising rock formation about 650 feet below the summit. We turned dubiously

[1] A cornice is a mass of snow and ice projecting over the lee side of a ridge. It is formed by wind blowing constantly in one direction.

41

to the north ridge, to see whether this might be less fraught with difficulty and danger. Cornice formations on this did not look quite so alarming; and, viewed from below, only the last 300 feet to the top appeared exceedingly steep, where the ridge petered out into the round snow-cap forming the summit. Maybe this difficulty could be overcome by traversing leftwards on to the north-east flank. From below, however, one could not say with any certainty what might, or might not, be possible up there.

Anyway, our first reconnaissance had revealed these critical sections on both ridges, difficult though it was from our view-point to assess one against the other. We finally agreed to leave the choice of the eventual route to the more experienced Terray. Although the Pongos question remained temporarily shelved, our reconnaissance had, rather unexpectedly, other repercussions. All the talk about possible ways of scaling the Pongos had so roused our climbing instincts that we, there and then, made up our minds to climb a mountain before Terray came on the scene, if only to get in some good training practice.

The question was simply which peak to select? In the group ot mountains to the north of the valley were several splendid virgin peaks. One of them, a nameless pyramid some 18,600 feet high, which we ourselves called the Chico Pongos,—or 'Little Pongos'— had challenging qualities quite equal to the Pongos massif. In fact, Little Pongos appeared to bristle with even more complications than big Pongos; so for the time being we directed our attention elsewhere.

Next to the Chico Pongos rose another massif with several independent peaks, all as yet unclimbed. In that respect, therefore, we had plenty of choice. According to the topographical chart, the highest was nearly 18,000 feet. After a short discussion, we decided to have a shot at this one. Viewed from below, it looked as though only the last section of the ridge, near the summit, might prove a really tough problem.

Our minds made up, there was now no holding us back. That very same day we started sorting out the climbing gear which we had been dragging along with us everywhere, seemingly to no purpose; and selected crampons, pitons and ropes. Leaving base camp on Wednesday, June 4th, we made our way towards the foot of the same glacier as before, intending to establish our first assault camp at an altitude of about 15,500 feet. During the trip we devoted considerable time to geological work, which necessitated our repeatedly crossing the streams running down from the glacier. De Booy was exasperatingly proficient in jumping nimbly across, quickly hopping from stone to stone, and invariably reaching the other side before I was even half-way across. I warned him repeatedly, if a little enviously, that these acrobatic tricks of his would sooner or later land him in trouble. And, true enough, as we started crossing for the third time, to my amusement, he slipped and sank to his waist in icy cold water. I simply couldn't resist pulling his leg about it and enlarging on the subject of recklessness always leading to trouble. But he took it all in such quiet, good part that my chaffing fell somewhat flat.

We arrived late that afternoon at the place chosen for our camp and pitched two little tents, each designed to hold two persons. One was for De Booy and me; the other for Eugenio, whom we had brought along. During our meal we debated whether or not to take him up any further. De Booy feared that his utter inexperience might render him more of a hindrance than a help, as he had never set foot on snow and ice until two days before, when he came with us on the glacier. My own view was that, on the contrary, it would be useful to have him with us, as any experience gained now might later prove valuable. Moreover, a group of three was better for crossing the snow-covered glacier ahead of us. If one member of the group fell into a crevasse it would be far less difficult for two to drag him out. One rescuer only would have much more of a job. This last argument won the day. In any case, we told ourselves, we

could always leave him behind if his presence occasioned any undue worry.

For days weather conditions had remained very settled. As we sat in front of our tents that evening talking about to-morrow's prospects, the sky became increasingly overcast. And all that night a glacial wind swept down, shaking our tents, while storms of hail rattled on the canvas. This certainly did not spell good weather for the trip. Moreover, more than once we were alarmed by the thunder of avalanches crashing down uncomfortably near at hand.

Yet, as we crawled out of our tents about six o'clock next morning, to our surprise the weather was fine. Only a few high clouds scudding across the sky reminded us of the stormy weather of the night. An hour sufficed for us to eat a frugal breakfast and get everything ready for the attack. As always, before a big climb, I was too tense to eat much. It was the first time for donning our nylon outer-clothing; and this in itself took a great deal of time. To put on boots proved a troublesome job, too, for they were frozen hard.

We left camp towards seven and the attempt began. The first part led over a seemingly endless moraine, strewn here and there with enormous blocks. Then the route went up sharply through a couloir. The terrain was not difficult, and we gained height rapidly. There was no talk of rest until about ten, by which time we had reached the edge of a sizeable snow-covered glacier. Here it was necessary to fix crampons and to rope up.

For our bearers we had brought out Grépon crampons (Simond), which had the merit of being adjustable to the size of their boots. On difficult terrain these crampons did not prove too good. Their points were rather short and afforded insufficient bite when soft snow covered a hard layer of ice.

Eugenio had a lot of trouble putting the climbing spikes under his boots. Fifteen minutes went by in measuring and fitting him properly. Then, the moment he was ready, without allowing ourselves any more time, we were off again, with De Booy in the lead.

This time we climbed slowly in an easterly direction over the glacier, which at first only sloped up gently. Here and there, great crevasses split the surface, but fortunately they were easily visible and easily avoided. After another hour the slope gradually became steeper and strong effort was required to maintain good speed. Our crampons started failing to grip, for the snow was deep and terribly dry. In particularly steep places we were constantly slipping back and sinking often to our thighs in snow. This is a tiresome slogging business at the best of times. Up at that rarefied altitude of 16,000 feet or more, it took all our lung capacity to keep going.

De Booy and I were naturally intrigued to discover how we reacted to lack of oxygen at high levels. To our great relief things turned out much better than we had expected. Even after a particularly trying passage it did not require more than a few moments to regain our breath.

Eugenio had done very well at first, but now the ascent was getting more difficult his morale fell lower and lower, and much precious time was lost in urging him on. It was nearly one before we reached a point about 500 feet below the summit. In front of us rose an almost perpendicular ice-wall, topped by a projecting cornice of formidable proportions. The wind, blowing continually in the same direction over the ridge, had so moulded this canopy of snow and ice that it now jutted out considerably over the lee-side.

It certainly did not look enticing. Our passage to the summit would take us beneath these masses of ice to a narrow ridge. From a small saddle, this ridge—at first sloping only slightly—went upwards right to the top. The saddle reached, we were able for the first time to scan the east flank and to confirm that it would be possible to scale the ridge. The steepness of the slope demanded such a degree of ice-technique manœuvring that it was inadvisable to take Eugenio any further. This was where knowledge and care were definitely essential.

When we told Eugenio that he could now untie the rope and re-

main in a safe place until we returned, his relief was unmistakable. He let us know that in any case he had not intended to go another step. What he could see of the climb ahead, as he expressed it in Spanish, 'was just too gruelling for the likes of him'.

Selecting a safe spot, we gave him strict instructions not to leave it on any account, as there were crevasses all around which were hardly visible owing to their deceptive coverings of snow. Any mooning about would put him in deadly peril. Once we had seen him comfortably placed, De Booy and I proceeded up the ridge, only to discover after the first few steps that this was also deceptive. There were numbers of snowed-in fissures which could only be detected by constant gouging with the axe.

Several rope-lengths up, the ridge began to narrow more and more. It also became quite a business to avoid the dangerous cornice. We were forced on to the steep east flank where the soft snow looked anything but trustworthy and aroused uneasy misgivings about avalanches. A little higher up, a tiny shelf gave us a welcome chance to stop for breath. Looking below we saw that Eugenio, in spite of all our warnings, was meandering round. De Booy bawled down that we wouldn't pay him his wages if he didn't immediately go back to his place. The threat had the desired effect.

From our shelf we saw that the ridge now tapered up to a slender crest—the crown of the cornice—and extended for about 100 feet right to the highest point, the summit of our mountain. As we had seen down below, this was precisely the place where the widest part of the overhanging canopy of snow jutted out over sheer space. It was overhanging some 16 feet, as far as we could tell. So we could only reach the summit by making another traverse along the face, which here sloped at a gradient of 50 degrees. All this made us wonder whether it would not be safer to turn back. Manœuvring just a little too deeply on that pitch could easily cause the mass of snow to start slithering down over the hard ice that undoubtedly lay beneath.

However, the mere thought of giving in at this stage touched our ambition too nearly. We agreed to carry on.

We should have liked to have hammered in some pitons for security, but they would have been useless in that deep powdery snow. One could hardly get a hold with the axe. We had to satisfy ourselves with a belay round an axe rammed in as deep as it would go. Even this was more of a moral support than anything else. By dint of the utmost care we negotiated the traverse without mishap. At 1.45 we reached the top—or, to be more precise, we approached it as closely as we dared with the point of the axe. The highest point was the bulge of the cornice, but as this jutted out several yards over the abyss, it was out of reach. Our altimeter gave a reading of about 18,400 feet. Years before, when the mountain was measured by the Germans, its height was shown on the map as 17,923 feet.

De Booy and I did not feel at all at ease, standing there precariously near the edge of the cornice. We allowed ourselves time only for fastening the Dutch flag on the shaft of an axe, for De Booy to hold it over the summit and for me to snap it with the camera. Then we started to return as fast as possible to the place where we had left Eugenio.

Descending first, I was about half-way down when an anxious moment occurred. My foot slipped and I had to put my full weight on the axe. It went right through the cornice! There suddenly gaped a hole through which the glacier hundreds of feet below could be seen. Whew! Shocks such as these make one go all weak at the knees. Fearful of hurtling with the cornice into the depths, I groped my way as quickly as possible down the east face, which now became steeper and steeper. It was only with the utmost concentration that we managed to negotiate the rest of it. Down at last, we were able to relax from the strain.

From below, Eugenio had been watching practically the whole operation. As we were clambering down the last few feet, he stood there waving his arms and shouting '*Viva Holanda! Viva Holanda!*'

Such a spontaneous outburst from this somewhat taciturn fellow took us completely by surprise, not to mention the effusive embrace we received on reaching safety. Unlocking myself from his welcoming arms, I had unholy pleasure in taking a leisurely photo of De Booy undergoing a similar but more drawn-out hug.

Eugenio had no regrets whatever that he had not accompanied us to the summit, but he was genuinely delighted at our success. We ourselves, looking upward, felt not a little pride in *our* peak. We both had now achieved the cherished ambition of every climber—to make a first ascent of a virgin peak without a guide. That this had been an entirely Dutch effort gave us added satisfaction. The attack itself had not proved so very difficult; even the last few hundred feet had not been fraught with too many technical difficulties. Nevertheless, the climb had distinctive features which we should not quickly forget. For one thing, we had come to grips with the most menacing problem confronting the climber in the Andes—the cornice.

After a brief respite we resumed the descent, Eugenio taking his place again in the middle of the rope. We went down rapidly over the glacier. The steep slopes, which had involved so much toil that morning, were now taken at glorious speed. Towards four we reached firm ground again, and thankful that the hard part was now over, we granted ourselves a well-earned rest.

We quenched our thirst by melting snow on a small meta-stove. Lumps of sugar, soaked with lemon-juice, went down fine. It was grand, too, after 'something attempted, something done', to be able to bask in the sun and talk it over. De Booy came up with all sorts of speculations about the dangers of that last face, and the chances of avalanches occurring in similar snow conditions. I, myself, had practically wiped out recollection of the steep face, except for that shuddering moment when the gaping hole had suddenly yawned through the cornice to disclose the glacier far below.

We reminded ourselves that our mountain had as yet no name.

48

Top R.: T. DE BOOY from Aerdenhout; 27 years of age; geologist; educated at Amsterdam University.

Middle L.: LIONEL TERRAY from Chamonix; 30 years of age; mountain guide and skiing instructor; second to climb north wall.

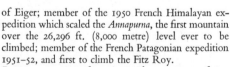

of Eiger; member of the 1950 French Himalayan expedition which scaled the *Annapurna*, the first mountain over the 26,296 ft. (8,000 metre) level ever to be climbed; member of the French Patagonian expedition 1951–52, and first to climb the Fitz Roy.

Bottom: C. G. EGELER from Amsterdam; 35 years of age; geologist on the staff of the Geological Institute of the Amsterdam University.

To climb a virgin peak reaching up to nearly 18,000 feet is all very well, but one had to call it something! It *had* to be christened. After endless discussion, we agreed to call it the Nevado Queshque after the valley below, the Quebrada Queshque. This would be in full accord with the custom in other parts of the Cordillera Blanca, where many mountains take their names from the valleys below. In this we were far less original than members of the Franco-Belgian expedition. After making a similar first ascent in the summer of 1951 in the northern portion of the Cordillera Blanca, they christened their newly-conquered peak, the Nevada Pisco, this being the name of a popular brand of Peruvian gin, of which they had consumed great quantities the day before. We, alas, could not think up anything so apt, our only liquids during the past few days having been tea and Milo malt drinks.

Late in the afternoon we decided it was time at last to go. We struggled to our feet and left the wonderful region of snow and ice. De Booy and Eugenio still had such funds of energy that they raced each other down. I followed more leisurely, my thoughts already focused on our next goal, the Pongos, now towering in front of us, its peak bathed in the setting sun.

Viewed from this side, the north-west face looked most uncompromising. I also gained a good impression of the difficulties that the south-west ridge would present in the shape of an enormous cornice, ice-plastered rock, steep ice. It wasn't going to be exactly child's play, getting up to the top.

This was by no means the first occasion that, descending one mountain, I had immediately fallen victim to the lure of the next. Indeed, it is invariably the same with me. The vanquished mountain has already been relegated to the background before I leave it. The Queshque lay behind, the Pongos before! Why look back?

The race between De Booy and Eugenio had one good result as far as I was concerned. By the time I arrived at base camp tea was already brewing; and not only tea. De Booy was busily preparing

D   49

Top: The Netherlands flag on the summit of an un-named mountain (17,923 feet). It was later christened the Nevado Queshque. *Bottom:* Eugenio embracing de Booy on his return

a victory feast—fried potatoes, minced meat, and delicious tinned fruit. This last, after a heavy day's climbing, was most welcome. Not that we didn't enjoy the other food, too. Nerves relaxed, appetite returned; and we made up for lost time by taking huge helpings of everything. Before we had finished eating, however, we were obliged to take shelter in our tents, for dusk brought a biting cold with it. Tucked snugly in our sleeping-bags, we munched happily away, then dropped off to sleep, only disturbed now and then by the thunder of some distant avalanche.

THE NEVADO PONGOS

After our success in climbing the Queshque, we felt eager to tackle a more difficult mountain. The following day, as we worked our way up the valley, bent on our geological mapping, our eyes kept straying at every break in operations to the virgin peaks in the vicinity, the Pongos and the Chico Pongos. They seemed positively to invite an attack. Suddenly the challenge proved too much for De Booy. He enthusiastically proposed that we should attempt the ascent of the Chico Pongos before Terray's arrival. Luckily he was open to reason when I pointed out that we really ought first to finish the geological work.

Meanwhile, we moved our headquarters back to base camp, still maintaining Camp 1, however, as it would certainly come in useful as an attack camp for the assault on the Pongos.

Blasido was sent down to Ticapampa to wait for Terray, whose arrival from Lima was expected at any moment. We thought he would want to join us at once, so that we could make a combined attempt on the Pongos without further loss of time.

The geological survey of the valley was finished on the evening of June 6th and we returned to base camp to await our French friend. Our anxiety about him grew with every minute. By supper

time, no one had appeared. So we climbed up a prominent crag, from where we could get a fine view down the valley. After some time we made out the figures of two riders a great distance off, slowly making their way through the swampy ground of the valley. For a moment we thought everything was in order, but, when the riders came nearer, we saw that it was Blasido and his brother-in-law, Leucadio. The latter had come along to look after the horses on the journey. Blasido told us, to our keen disappointment, that Terray had not arrived that morning, neither had anything been heard from him. This was a blow. According to our calculations Terray should have arrived a day or so ago. His continued absence now threatened to upset our carefully-timed programme and waste much valuable time.

After a short debate it was decided that De Booy and Blasido should set off first thing next morning and stay in Ticapampa until Terray arrived. If he did not appear in a few days' time, De Booy would contact the French legation at Lima, where Terray would certainly report on landing. I, meanwhile, would remain and use my time in writing articles for the press. Perhaps I might also have the opportunity to make a detailed investigation of one of the granodiorite contacts in the neighbourhood.

All this proved unnecessary. When De Booy arrived in Ticapampa hot foot the next afternoon, he found Terray already there, snugly ensconced with our inestimable host, Mr. Kroupnitzky. But comfortable though he was, Terray longed to tackle those lofty snow-capped peaks he had glimpsed the previous noon during his journey over the Cordillera Negra. Despite travel weariness, Terray wanted to set off there and then for the Queshque valley. The indomitable De Booy, who had already done six hours on horseback, was also game. So they started off, and late that same evening arrived at base camp.

I, myself, had crept nice and early that evening into my sleeping bag, reconciled to the thought that several days were bound to go

by before I saw my fellow-members. A few hours later I was startled from a light sleep by something that sounded ominously like an Indian war-cry. It was a howl set up by the boisterous Terray. According to De Booy he had ridden his beast for hours at a fierce gallop over a track which, at the best, was not too safe.

We greeted each other warmly. It seemed ages since the previous year when we had said good-bye in Chamonix, and it was great to have this reunion in far-off Peru. This was the turning-point in the expedition—the mountaineering part would now be on with a vengeance. The dream was about to be realized.

As we sat together in the tent, Terray could hardly wait to announce that he had a big surprise in store for us. He had actually been able to bring along a marvellous 16 mm. cine-camera and a lovely miniature camera equipped with telephoto lens. This expensive apparatus had been kindly loaned to him by the French Himalayan Committee. Moreover, he had himself bought a great quantity of coloured film. This was excellent news. Our own film camera had fallen in the water whilst crossing a river on one of our surveys, and we were afraid to rely on it any more. It was a heavy cumbersome thing, impossible to take on difficult climbs, whereas Terray's apparatus was light in weight. Needless to say, he was keen to take it on every climb the expedition made. Actually, we could not have been more grateful. After the expedition when our own films were developed, every single shot was found to be spoiled owing to the fouling of the lens in the water. The photos taken with Terray's apparatus were perfect. Thanks to him, we were able to bring home a most satisfactory film of the whole affair.

During the next few days Terray was constantly being chaffed by us about the way in which he set about filming. He did it with a most unexpected seriousness and precision. Details of the time, place, and visibility of every shot were carefully entered in a book. De Booy, knowing Terray, bluntly said: 'Oh, all this won't last very long!'—and he was right.

While Terray told us about his journey, Eugenio and I were busy getting supper ready for him and De Booy. For this special occasion I selected a tin of tasty pea-soup with boiled bacon. Unfortunately, it did not turn out such a good idea after all, for both of them were terribly bilious during the night. This was certainly learning the hard way that one had rigidly to avoid heavy food and fats when at high level.

On waking the next day, Lionel had other symptoms, indicating that his transition within the last few days from sea-level up to nearly 14,000 feet had been somewhat rapid. He was suffering from headache; but this did not prevent him from coming along with us to Camp 1. Accompanied by the two bearers, we went in leisurely fashion up the valley to the little camp at the foot of the glacier. De Booy and I, already familiar with the way and the mountain scenery found the journey to Camp 1 just a pleasant walk. Terray, on the other hand, had his eyes fixed on our goal, the Pongos, towering like a mighty fortress over the valley.

We told Terray how our first reconnaissance had revealed that from this side there seemed to be two possible assault routes to the Pongos pyramid. We could take either the north ridge or the south-west ridge. The northerly route might be the simpler, but we had deferred decision and the location of an attack camp until he arrived on the scene.

The nearer Terray approached the mountain, and the closer he scanned the ridges, the more enthusiastic he became. Lower in the valley his view of the peak had been too limited to get a proper perspective. But now it became clear to him that our chosen objective was one it would be foolish to underestimate. He shared our view that we should really need to gird our loins if we wished to bring this venture to a successful conclusion.

After our midday meal, headache or no headache, nothing could stop Terray from accompanying me up the glacier. He simply had to climb up high and get a good look through the field-glasses at

that northerly route. On reaching 16,000 feet, we devoted over an hour to this reconnaissance. Terray confirmed our opinion that the north ridge, taken as a whole, looked easier than the south-west; but, just as I was taking it for granted that he had definitely decided on the north route, he startled me with 'And yet we will take the south-west route'. I asked his reasons.

'Take a good look through these glasses,' he replied. 'About half-way up that north ridge you'll see an indentation—a sort of cleft—breaking the line of the *arête*. From here, of course, one cannot say what it's really like up there. But it strikes me as likely to turn out a tough proposition. It certainly looks as though we might be held up indefinitely at that point by all sorts of difficulties. We might perhaps have to drive in a heck of a lot of pitons, all taking an enormous amount of time. Why should we risk having to abandon things half-way, if another route *is* possible, even though it may look a bit more difficult. We must regard the extra difficulties as just healthy exercise, *n'est-ce pas?*'

In face of such logic, words failed me. I felt rather abashed, too, that De Booy and I had completely overlooked that cleft in the north ridge. I drew Terray's attention, however, to those excessively steep rocks high up on the south-west ridge and asked whether these might not also prove insuperable. On this score Terray was less pessimistic. He doubted whether it would be possible to climb up these rocks to the ridge, but he thought we might be able to avoid them by a detour along one of the faces of the mountain, although a traverse in the west face was hardly possible, owing to the grim giant cornice.

Ah, well—one had to take mountains as they are! A first ascent of a peak of this class meant that one simply had to leave a lot to luck. As Terray put it: 'Je ne sais comment on passera, mais on passera quand même!'

De Booy, back in camp, had been eagerly awaiting our return. The moment he heard Terray's decision he began getting every-

thing ready for the next day. He sorted out equipment and provisions for about four days and divided them among the rucksacks. Terray wanted to get as high up the west face as possible and to establish a second assault camp on the steep glacier below the ridge. To reach this point it would be necessary for both porters to climb a fairly steep ice-fall.

When I explained this, Eugenio made a long face. The climbing of the Queshque had impressed him deeply. He now realized how dangerous the great ice slopes could be, and how crevasses lurked treacherously in the glaciers. When I pointed out the proposed route up the Pongos, all he could mutter was: '*Terrible, Señor doctor.* . . . *Terrible!*' But Blasido did nothing but grin. He had not set foot on ice in his whole life, but the spirit of adventure had now too much sway for him to be afraid of anything.

We decided to leave one of the two-man tents standing in Camp I. In Camp 2 use would be made of the two Himalayan tents Lionel Terray had brought from France. One of these was of the Nanda Devi type, designed to hold three persons. The other was a two-man nylon tent that had kindly been put at our disposal by the French Himalayan Committee. It had been used on the Annapurna and we looked forward to using it ourselves for the first time with considerable respect.

At ten o'clock on June 9th we left Camp I, and slowly made our way, heavily laden, through endless scree towards the lower *tongue* of the glacier. The loads were a foretaste of the weights we should have to shoulder in the coming weeks. It was a case of carrying tents, sleeping bags, provisions, cooking equipment, and all essential clothing up to high altitudes. We also had to take a great number of ice-pitons.

On reaching the foot of the glacier, we roped up in two groups. Terray and I took Eugenio, who was carrying the heaviest load; while De Booy took Blasido under his wing. On our climbs we always used two 200-foot nylon ropes, one white and the other

orange. The rope was only 8 mm. in thickness, so it could be used for rappels and for roping up (*Corde d'attache*). The colour contrast came in most useful when both ropes were in use together. Nylon rope is indeed far superior to manilla or hemp rope. It is only half the weight and always remains supple and pliable, even when frozen.

Sketch of the area around the Pongos.
Route up the south-west ridge of the Pongos.

We immediately met with several fairly steep passages, obliging the porters to make full use of their crampons, which they did at first somewhat awkwardly. Terray showed them how to bend

their ankles and how to dig all the spikes of their crampons evenly in the ice at each step. We slowly toiled up and up, through a confusion of crevasses, across the ice-fall. Here and there Terray kept cutting steps in the ice to ease the way for the porters. Once, on a steep incline, Eugenio started slipping and had to be held on the rope. Surprisingly enough, this had a most salutary effect. When the bearers saw how easily it was done, they realized that they were running no very great risks, and they consequently acquired far more self-reliance. Blasido, in particular, showed himself most adaptable after a time.

It soon became evident that we had topped the 16,500-ft. mark, for slowly but surely we began to get breathless. Any difficult manœuvring seemed to demand a disproportionate effort. As we climbed, the mountain scenery became more and more beautiful, particularly the Queshque. Down below, it had not looked at all imposing, but here its real stature was revealed. The sight gave De Booy and me a definite feeling of satisfaction. Lionel had hitherto not paid much attention to our account of the ascent of this mountain, but now he evinced keen interest in our climbing route. The Chico Pongos, too, looked most impressive from here, making us wonder whether we could possibly manage to tackle it before we left for another part of the range.

Towards one o'clock we reached a place which was not quite so steep and appeared suitable for the pitching of Camp 2. The altimeter registered 17,320 feet. We were now well up the glacier and directly below the ridge. It was clear that, a few hundred feet higher up, the technicalities would be too complicated for us to take our bearers any further.

The day was beautifully warm. For that matter, the weather so far had been very kind to us, although towards the east thick banks of clouds were gathering over the Amazon plain.

As always, the setting up of the camp took considerable time. Using duralumin spades, we dug out two level platforms on which

to pitch our tents. In doing this we had to take care not to leave anything lying on the ground, for the slope was such that any loose objects had a way of sliding away and disappearing in a jiffy into the depths. This happened to Eugenio, to his chagrin, when he let a spade fall. Mouth open in astonishment, he saw it slide swiftly down, and vanish a few moments later into a crevasse 100 feet down. It led to a true Gallic scolding from Lionel. The worthy Eugenio understood not a word of French, but obviously grasped the general drift.

When fixing the tents one also had to guard against possible uprooting by wind. We therefore buried down the sides of the tents, all along their lengths. Under Terray's eagle eye it was three before everything was arranged just so. He, of course, had done this sort of thing scores of times before. Two orange-coloured tents now stood firmly and proudly on the face. When reading books about expeditions to the Himalayas and the Andes we had often looked longingly at photos of similar encampments. Now we ourselves had such a camp, somewhere on some unknown mountain.

While the others were busy setting up the camp, I was seeing to the cooking, first of all melting a lot of snow. At that height, low air pressure caused boiling-point to be much lower than at sea-level, so cooking proved a long and tedious business. What is more, the moment I did succeed in melting a saucepan-full of water, up would come some member of the party asking for a drink, and not being satisfied until the pan was emptied. Finally, after an hour and a half, a good quantity of tea was ready. The others had finished their jobs, too, so we all sat down comfortably to our midday meal.

We sat basking in the sun for hours that afternoon, enjoying the lovely scenery. We did some filming and chatted endlessly about tomorrow's venture. As always, the Peruvian day proved too short. About 5 o'clock the sun went behind a neighbouring mountain and at once a chilling night cold descended. We were forced to seek the shelter of our tents and creep into our sleeping bags. We

actually cooked supper in the tent. The great advantage of the Nanda Devi type is that it leaves ample space at both ends. In one end rucksacks, boots, ropes, etc., can be dumped, whilst at the other end there is room for cooking. During the preparation of the meal there was a bit of an upset. The lighted candle was placed near a flask which had no stopper in it. When Terray asked for something to drink, I thought the flask contained water and handed it over; but a few seconds later, I realized that it was anything but water. Only after hectic minutes of spluttering and cursing, did we gather that I had given him petrol to drink. He went right off the Gallic deep-end, particularly about leaving the open petrol flask so near to the candle.

'You fatheads! Have you gone mad?' he choked indignantly. 'Do you think it funny to spend the night up here at 17,000 feet, beside a burnt-out tent?'

He could not have been more right. It was plain that only nerve would help us out of this situation. When De Booy coolly said: 'But surely petrol is for burning, so why all the fuss?' Terray was so taken aback that further words failed him. But, from then on, whenever we were cooking, Terray constantly glanced uneasily in our direction, obviously making sure everything was in order.

The candle went out at half-past seven, but none of us could get to sleep for a number of reasons. The cloudbanks which had been piling up that afternoon on the east side of the Cordillera, had now increased considerably. Even in the dark we could see how the Pongos summit was enveloped in black cloud, and we knew from experience that this boded ill. When, after a few hours it began to snow lightly, we feared the weather prospects for the morning would be none too good.

At 4.30 next morning we were awakened by Terray's alarm watch. Our first thoughts were of the weather. We flung open the tent flap. One look was sufficient! During the night the tents had become partly snowed-under, but the bad weather was over. The

sky was perfectly clear, except for a few clouds on the far eastern horizon. The surrounding mountains were silhoutted with razor sharpness against the starry sky.

According to our estimate, six inches of snow had fallen in the night, but correct measurement was difficult as the wind had swept it into thick drifts. For a time I thought that this, in itself, might prevent our going on with the climb, but Terray reckoned we could safely proceed, even though the snow might well prove an extra hindrance.

How terribly cold it had been during that night at the 17,000-ft. altitude could be seen from our sleeping bags. They were frozen here and there to the tent walls and had to be dislodged with force. The thermometer stood at minus 10° C.

Early rising in piercing cold to begin a hard climb is always something of a dubious pleasure. On the one hand, one wants to be up good and early to get under way; on the other hand, one shivers at the cold and at the thought of all the self-imposed privations ahead. On that particular morning all three of us were deplorably sluggish. We tried to push responsibility for getting breakfast on Eugenio and Blasido, so that we could snooze a little longer in the lovely warmth of our sleeping bags. Unfortunately, our deep designs went awry. When we shouted at the other tent the only reply was—a groan. Terray and I agreed that De Booy ought to go out and see what was wrong. He naturally quibbled about this, but we argued that as he lay in the centre of the tent it was easiest for him to creep out. This finally won the day. A few minutes later he came back with the news that both bearers were down with mountain-sickness. They had splitting headaches and declined to come out of their sleeping bags. It was odd that we, who were accustomed to living at sea-level, should already have become completely acclimatized after only one month, while these fellows who had spent their whole lives 10,000 feet up, should have succumbed after only one night at the 17,000-ft. altitude. A few APC tablets

and some encouraging words were all we could give them. Now that we had to get our own breakfast, there was little time to spare. In any case it was imperative to have a quick hot drink to counter-act the intense cold, so De Booy prepared the Milo malt, whilst I got the porridge ready.

Towards dawn we were all set, crampons on, for the big climb. With Terray in the lead, then me, and De Booy last, we slowly made our way up the steep snow-covered glacier to the edge of the south-west ridge.

The great adventure was on! Our target glittered aloft—a mountain untrodden by the foot of man. We were making our way into the unknown, where none knew what technical snags awaited. Compared with the climb now before us, the Queshque ascent had been child's play. Would we again be successful?

I felt keyed up, as before an examination. Happily this sensation soon disappeared, and I came again under the spell of the unknown, the call of adventure. After all, the greater the effort demanded, the greater the ultimate satisfaction.

The Pongos did not leave us guessing long. As soon as we reached the ridge serious difficulties began. Just as on the Queshque, this ridge had an enormous cornice poised over the west flank, making it impossible for us to follow the crest. We were obliged to traverse on to the south face, which we found to be ex-ceedingly steep here, sloping at an angle of fifty degrees. We had to get used to it though, for the abyss over which we manœuvred was breath-taking: a sheer drop of 5,000 feet to the glacier below. The snow was deep and powdery, as on the Queshque. De Booy and I had then feared avalanche dangers and had climbed in con-tinual dread lest the whole mass of snow started sliding away under our feet. Terray reassured us on that point. This particular sort of snow was, he assured us, quite safe. However, he admitted being impressed by the gaping void below us. We had to exer-cise the greatest possible care and to omit no security precaution.

For two long hours the way led along this tilted snowy slope, two hours of horizontal traversing, hardly winning a foot of height. For most of the distance we traversed with our faces towards the slope, anchoring ourselves at every step with the axe well driven into the deep snow above our heads. Rapid progress was out of the question and in the whole two hours we only covered a few hundred yards.

Then a little break in the ridge gave us hope of being able to reach the crest. It was a good place to take a short rest. De Booy took the opportunity to film the ridge higher up, and particularly the wind-scattered wisps of mist over the mountain.

From this point we gained another view of the west face. Far below were the small tents of Camp 2, where one of the porters was pottering about. He was such a speck in the landscape that we couldn't make out whether it was Blasido or Eugenio. Perhaps the mountain-sickness was on the wane. I shouted—and lo and behold, the porter seemed to spot us, for he waved back.

During this short breather we had a bite of something to eat, then on we went. Almost immediately new problems arose, forcing us again on the steep flank of the ridge, where the gradient was even sharper than before. This time, however, we clawed our way straight upwards instead of sideways. The first few hundred feet were telling. Again and again we leaned worn out against the wall, gasping for breath.

After hours of uninterrupted work we saw that the arête[1], now not far above us, was blocked by a rock buttress extending over both flanks of the mountain. This was the dreaded obstacle we had discussed so much since our first reconnaissance in the valley. There was no doubt about it: we had now reached a ticklish stage. Further ascent of the south-west ridge depended on whether, by some means or other, we could get by this rock barrier.

At first, from a distance, it seemed possible. After another fifteen

[1] *Arête*—sharp ascending ridge of a mountain.

minutes, however, we reached a saddle at the foot of the rocks, and took a closer look. They looked most unpleasant. Most of them were overhanging and covered with verglas, difficulties which invariably face the climber among the peaks of the Cordillera Blanca.

In the Alps it is often advisable to follow the rock and avoid the steep ice-ridges: in the Peruvian mountains it is just the reverse. Whenever possible one avoids the rocks which are mostly ice-covered. As Terray had prophesied two days previously, a traverse along the face was necessary. Climbing the precipitous rock barriers would entail the driving in of innumerable pitons, to say nothing of other complications.

We now had to find the best possible route for our detour. A traverse to the left on to the west face was absolutely impossible, for the way up the wall was blocked for hundreds of feet by massive overhanging shelves of ice. Even if it had been technically possible to force our way through, the risks were too overwhelming. Now that the sun had become more powerful, large and small chunks of the ice shelving were continually breaking off, and thundering into the depths below. They were falling right over the route we would have to traverse.

The remaining possibility was a traverse along the south flank. We would have to start this low down, for here again overhanging masses of ice prevented rapid passage upwards and it would be necessary to pass under them before any height could be gained. Negotiating this passage, Terray revealed his great gifts of leadership. As soon as he had decided to try this way, he advanced unhesitatingly, but with the utmost care, across the ice-slope still separating us from the rocks.

After a few minutes he reached the nearest rock-band. It was a tense moment. We watched him trying to find a hold, but, as we had surmised, the rock was completely coated with ice. The lower reaches, against which he stood, bulged slightly. The first attempt to pass failed, and Terray was obliged to let himself slide back on the

63

ice-steep. At the second attempt he succeeded, after a struggle, in passing the critical spot and pulled himself up a few yards. For a brief moment he stood there, a dark silhouette against the clear sky. Then he disappeared round the corner. De Booy and I, who had been breathlessly following his every movement, felt tenser than ever, now he had vanished from view. What would he find? Would there be a way up the face?

In the silence that followed, Terray's progress could only be judged by the slow paying-out of the rope, which I had belayed round my axe. Then, to our relief, came the sound of the hammer, telling us that he had at last found a foothold and was driving in a piton. We knew we could follow! A moment later his red beret came in sight round the rock. He shouted to me to avoid the over-hanging rock by traversing the sloping face as low down as possible.

With a last enjoinder to De Booy to secure me well, I followed Terray's track across the ice-slope. I had closely watched his method of tackling the difficulties ahead, so the going was not too tough. In order to get a better hold of the slippery rock, however, I took off my gloves. Thank goodness the passage did not last long, for the touch of the icy stone immediately numbed the fingers of both hands. Once around the bend I could see Terray several yards above me on the face. From here, one could plainly see what lay before: it was, to say the least of it, discouraging—the most abrupt steep I had ever encountered. From where Terray stood, we had to climb some 300 feet up ice pitched at an angle of about 65 degrees and covered with deep powdery snow. We normally traversed terrain such as this, but further detours on the face of the mountain were out of the question. There was nothing for it, but to go straight up.

Cautiously climbing up to Terray, I reached the piton and stopped a second to get breath. Then I shouted to De Booy to come on, and slowly hauled in the rope. Meanwhile Terray left the little shelf and began to work his way upwards. Slowly but surely he

64

The Chico Pongos (18,635 feet)

went, driving in his axe as far above his head as he could, then hauling himself up on it. He continually sank to his thighs in the soft deep snow. Time and time again he tried to find footholds, but each time he kept sliding back a bit. It was a Herculean task and took every ounce of breath, but—he progressed.

It took him quite fifteen minutes to climb the first hundred feet. Then, as I couldn't let out any more rope, Terray hacked out a little level place in the face and called to me to follow up as fast as possible. The track thus made, it was somewhat easier for me, although at each step up I found myself slithering back a bit. I was just about all in when I managed to join Terray on the small platform. There was little left of the original track when it came to De Booy's turn to come up. He, too, had the greatest difficulty in making headway.

It took three more rope lengths, repeating the selfsame process, before we completed this laborious, exhausting passage. It lasted a good hour, but finally the three of us straddled the ridge, feeling that we had done a good job of work and cherishing a faint hope that perhaps the worst was now over. At any rate it was now possible to go up the crest of the *arête*. After a time, trouble started again. This time we had to deflect on to the west flank, where the slope was just as steep as the one just negotiated.

But there is an end to everything. At half-past twelve we finally caught sight of the summit. There was just one more nasty piece in front to overcome, involving getting on the east face, where a snow field slanted up to the top. It was necessary to cross over the ridge, but this was covered by an abominably wide cornice, out of which we would have to chop a part before we could go on.

Where we had now landed was indeed a tricky spot, giving the impression it could collapse at any moment. It was a case of touch and go—all too easily could one be carried down with the falling ice. Terray went to work with the greatest caution. Climbing slowly to where blue ice showed through here and there, he hacked

E

The Nevado Pongos (18,737 feet). De Booy points out the proposed line of attack to Eugenio

away a passage through the overhanging cornice and then disappeared over the crest. De Booy and I feverishly waited. Only the slow pay-out of the rope showed that Terray was still moving. A few minutes later we heard him shout, and it was my turn to go over the top. Warily I followed in Terray's track. Arriving at the crest I paused a moment for breath—only to be immediately challenged by our leader.

'Qu'est ce que tu fais là, Kees?' he yelled.

'Moi je souffle un peu!' I gasped.

'Ah, mon vieux, tu peux souffler à n'importe quel endroit, mais ici . . . jamais! Ce passage est drôlement dangereux!'

These words stirred me at once into activity and I hastily descended the other side of the *arête* on to a snowy slope. From here the way to the summit lay clear, but this fiercely steep snow-field took full toll of energy and lung power. Panting for breath, we toiled up the last few yards.

The summit was reached!

It was one o'clock when the French and Netherlands flags, fastened to the shafts of our axes, fluttered fraternally side by side on the 18,737-ft. high summit of the Pongos, the loftiest peak of the entire southern massif.

Victory was ours, and the first big climbing success of our Andes expedition had been secured. In past years I often used to ask myself what mountaineers actually did when, after an arduous and perilous climb, they finally reached the top of a virgin peak. Now we ourselves were sitting on a summit rising to 18,737 feet above level ground.

What *did* we do? Well, we looked around, but were much too spent at first to enjoy the view. We took snaps and tried, with some aversion, to eat something. Actually, the feeling of triumph came much later on, after we had tackled the descent with all its hazards.

The view was, of course, superb. We could see the Cordillera

Blanca stretching for tens of miles on both sides of us. In the south reared the Caullaraju massif, not particularly impressive. But definitely awesome was the mighty silhouette of the Yerupaja, towering imperiously still further south in the Huashhuash Cordillera. Our Queshque mountain lay far below us. It now looked an insignificant hill, belonging to the past.

And the future . . . ? In the far distance a fantastic ice-pyramid towered head and shoulders above its neighbours. It was the mighty Huantsán, which we were shortly to challenge. After to-day's success such an attack seemed at least to be a shade more conceivable.

There was little charm about the Pongos summit, which we had reached with so much toil and stress. It was big and level enough for a football field. The mountain formed, as it were, a broad dome with steep sides.

About 1,400 feet below us lay Camp 2. We saw a bearer moving about outside the tent. Lower still, at the head of the Queshque valley, we made out the solitary tent of Camp 1. Far in the distance, hardly discernible to the naked eye, stood the big tent of our base camp. An *arriero* was due to arrive that day with horses and donkeys for the journey down the valley. He certainly would stare to find the camp completely deserted. We stared, too, through the glasses, but could see no animals in sight.

I asked Terray how he felt. The verve with which he had been able to lead us up the peak was absolutely staggering, when one recalled that he had allowed himself such little time to get acclimatized. On June 3rd he was still in France; on June 5th in Lima at sea-level, and to-day, June 10th, here he was up at the 18,737-ft. level, on the lofty summit of the Pongos. The only thing that bothered him was a slight headache. Truly a unique achievement, of which Terray himself was a little proud; and when we so roundly expressed our admiration, he could not help showing his gratification.

With night falling early in the Peruvian Andes, time was now

growing short. After twenty minutes on the summit we began the descent, and, as is often the case with steep ice, found it more beset with difficulty than the ascent, requiring the utmost concentration. We were, in fact, so engrossed that none of us noticed the weather taking a turn for the worse. Whilst resting on the summit we had, it is true, eyed with distrust the dark clouds heaped over the Amazon plain, little dreaming they would so soon become a source of danger. We took quick notice when the first hailstones clattered on our heads. We were still on the ridge, just above the band of rocks which had proved so troublesome that morning during the ascent. All at once the entire mountain was shrouded in mist and we could hardly see more than a few feet ahead.

The thunder roared in the distance and, according to Terray, he felt the electricity in the air in his hair. Later on, when safe and sound in camp, we pulled Terray's leg unmercifully about this remark, for he is nearly bald.

At that moment, however, the information did nothing to cheer us up. Severe weather overtaking us on this *arête* could have ugly consequences. We particularly had to guard against over-hastiness. Every precaution had to be taken. No security measure overlooked. In such difficult terrain it was madness to try to go any faster. Each of us therefore carried on as calmly as possible, concentrating vigorously on the work, and not wasting any time in needless breathers. No more jokes were cracked. No unnecessary words exchanged; only the curt phrases needed for rope manipulation.

Going down the exceedingly steep slope which had taken over an hour to climb that morning, we found that the descent fortunately took less time than the ascent, for we could allow ourselves to slide down secured by a rammed-in axe, without bothering too much about foot support. At last we came to the piton hammered in earlier on by Terray. This could now be made to serve for the *rappel*, or descent by rope, over the rock formations and ice-wall. And now, as he began to speed things up, Terray kept on breathing

hard, always a sign with him of great tension. Mist still enveloped the mountain, but the hailstones had turned to snow.

As soon as the rope had been passed through the ring I went down, secured by Lionel. First I had to clear the rocks. Then, on the steep ice below, I had to bear to the left as much as possible in order to reach the saddle and not land in the abyss. It nearly went wrong. My left leg suddenly went deeply into a crevasse deceptively covered with snow, and I lost my balance. With contracting heart I swung sideways some twenty yards or more on the taut rope, and finally came to rest hanging in space. Terray, following my motions from above, began swearing—a natural enough reaction.

I reproached myself bitterly. Up to then, everything had gone splendidly, and now I had to make this stupid mistake. With some difficulty I pulled myself together and a few minutes later secured a firm foothold on the saddle near the foot of the rocks. I could breathe again. The manœuvre, in spite of that nerve-racking moment, had turned out all right.

A little later the others landed safely, too, and we treated ourselves to a short rest. As we took a last glance at the ridge, the sun broke through the clouds. The greatest hazards were behind us—and so apparently was the dirty weather.

We were able to move down quickly from the saddle to the place where we had earlier eaten. Gradually I had grown really tired. We had been on the go for ten whole hours, hours of severe mental and physical strain, and I couldn't say that I looked forward to that tricky traverse across the south-west face, which that morning had lasted all of two hours. But cheers! Terray had other plans. Whilst we had been resting there, he had been peering below and now he announced, to our relief, that he had discovered another route which would cut out that tiresome traverse. He intended, he said, going down the west face.

He accordingly forged ahead to see if there were any insuperable obstacles. Soon there came a shout from below, a sign for us to fol-

low. Down we climbed over sharply tilted snow-fields, reaching—via a steep ice-slope—the snow-covered glacier. This route was undoubtedly simpler than the way we had climbed. Terray explained that it had been impossible to detect it from below as a projecting cornice obstructed the view. When in doubt he thought it better to be sure than sorry.

The new route was not only easier, but time-saving. Reaching the glacier, we saw the tents quite close at hand. With only three-quarters of an hour to go before sunset, we arrived safely back in Camp 2. Terray had careered on ahead, and we saw him now being embraced and congratulated by one of the bearers. It was Eugenio, welcoming us with hot tea and lemon. Before we could drink it, De Booy and I had to submit to a hearty embrace as well.

Eugenio, who had fortunately recovered from his mountain-sickness, told us that he had been able to follow most of our climb. Blasido, on the other hand, was still wretchedly ill and, according to Eugenio, had been vomiting blood. On further inquiry we learned that Blasido had suffered from his lungs in the past, having contracted silicosis during a period of mine work. He lay there, deep in his sleeping bag, too ill to stand. It seemed imperative to get him away before he lost more strength, but it was of course impossible to do anything so late that day. Descent of the steep glacier with a sick man was out of the question in the dark. We decided that De Booy should take him below early next morning. Terray, Eugenio, and I would break camp and follow on more slowly, carrying the heavy gear. After searching in our medicine chest, we gave Blasido some tablets against bronchitis. If they didn't do good, well, they couldn't do any harm. We also gave him a strong sleeping draught in the hope that it would ensure a good night's rest.

Blasido's illness naturally damped our spirits, but we could not help feeling satisfied with ourselves that evening. The ascent of the Pongos had gone extraordinarily well, notwithstanding the fact that the climb had been far tougher than expected.

De Booy and I sought Terray's verdict on the climb. We learned that he regarded the problems of the last 600 feet or so to the top as quite comparable with any of the truly difficult ice-climbs in the Alps, even if one only took into account the exposed nature and general delicacy of the exceptionally narrow ice-ridge up which we had to force our way to the summit.

Blasido's condition was still far from satisfactory next day, but luckily he was able to move. Under De Booy's kindly care, he set off down the glacier. Some hours later Terray and I followed with the heavily laden Eugenio. It wasn't too easy at various places and more than once the falling Eugenio had to be held on the rope by Terray. On the whole Eugenio seemed to be enjoying himself; and this made me more hopeful for the future.

When we reached the foot of the glacier, Terray and I left him behind, while we went down the slope at top speed. Terray got ahead of me and no matter how I exerted myself, I simply could not catch up. However, near a spot where we had to cross the glacier stream, he waited for me. Jumping from stone to stone over the stream, Terray—for one who usually was so surefooted—now seemed unsure of himself. Half-way across, he slipped. So, for the second time during our stay in the Pongos massif, I was fated to see a companion immersed in the icy water. The lurid language Terray used is, of course, unrepeatable.

De Booy welcomed us in Camp 1 with lashings of hot tea. Later that day we made our leisurely way down to base camp. There we met the *arriero* who was to bring up pack-horses by June 10th, and who, miracle of miracles, had kept his part of the agreement. Thus it was possible to break camp next day and start back to Ticapampa. Wending our way down the winding valley, from the bank of a lake, we caught a last dazzling view of our mountain, rising majestically over the vale. Then we rounded a bend—the Pongos adventure was behind us.

With this climb one of the chief mountaineering aims of our

Andes expedition had been realized. Not only that. The two ascents we had made were ideal training for what lay ahead.

But what *did* the future have in store?

That was the question De Booy and I kept asking ourselves. It was one to which only Terray could give the answer. His would be the decision whether we should be justified in attempting the Huantsán, our ultimate goal—the mountain which they said in the valley was unclimbable.

We did not have to put the question after all. That selfsame evening, as we sat by a cheerful fire in the Kroupnitzkys' living-room in Ticapampa, Terray suddenly said: 'I think three days will suffice to get everything ready. We will start for the Huantsán on June 15th.'

THE NEVADO HUANTSÁN

ON THE WAY TO THE MOUNTAIN

From the moment Terray made his decision, everything centred on our new objective—the Huantsán. But we knew very little about this mountain, except that it was the highest unclimbed peak in the whole Cordillera Blanca. Schneider, a member of two Austro-German expeditions to the Andes, wrote *inter alia* about the ascent possibilities:

'The highest peak of the southern group, the Nevado Huantsán, is perhaps at the same time the finest unscaled mountain of the range. It is beautiful to look at from all sides, besides being conspicuous for its defiant faces. It offers only two possible approaches: the north ridge, long and difficult, has the advantage of direction. It is much more easily and comfortably reached from the east than from the west. The second possibility is the south ridge, which is reached through the Quebrada Rajucolta. Perhaps this is an easy route when snow conditions are good. There is only one questionable part in it, the sheer drop from the summit structure towards the col between it and its southern subsidiary peak.'

Members of the Austro-German expeditions made only one attack on the Huantsán. In 1939, Rohrer and Schweitzer tried to get at the mountain from the south-west via the Rurec valley, but quickly discovered that it was not the best route, for the way upwards was barred by a spur, the climbing of which constituted an ascent in itself. After studying the mountain from a point at the

18,000-ft. level, they came to the conclusion that the north ridge offered the best possibilities after all, even though it looked by no means simple.

No other attempts were subsequently made on the Huantsán, which was regarded by everyone familiar with the Andes as one of the toughest propositions in the Cordillera Blanca.

When our plans to make an attempt on the Huantsán were published in the world press, we received a report that an American expedition from the Californian University had also chosen this mountain as its objective. The question was who would be first, and, what was perhaps more to the point, who would be able to find the best attack route.

Though the photographs did not give much to go on, we had, long before, discussed at great length the assault possibilities from all aspects. We did not agree with the conclusion reached by Schneider that, given good snow conditions, the south ridge might offer good possibilities. Careful study of the various photographs convinced us that the precipitous part between the southern subsidiary peak and the main summit presented difficulties of a practically insuperable nature. We formed the opinion that no detour was possible round the rocks, and were fairly certain, too, that these would be completely sheathed in ice. Everything indicated that enormous technical difficulties would have to be faced up there at the high altitude of over 20,000 feet.

As against this, the northern approach was admittedly long. But, as far as we could make out from the photographs, it was not excessively steep in any part. Rather than run the risk of being obliged to turn back by insurmountable difficulties at a great height, we preferred to face the length of the latter route. Thus it was that our eventual choice fell on the northern *arête* of the Huantsán. This decided, our next problem was to find the best approach to it. Here we did allow ourselves to be guided by Schneider's view that the easiest access was from the east.

We made up our minds to move our porters and all our gear by lorry to the little village of Chavin on the eastern side of the chain. From there we should be able to get into the range with pack-animals and to reach the foot of the Huantsán massif through the Caruascancha valley. It later turned out that we had picked a good, but by no means the best, line of approach. The shortest route to a good assault base on the mountain is actually from the west through the Shallap valley. From Huaraz, access can be gained to this valley in a few hours on horseback. At its higher reaches the valley meets a steep but climbable glacier, over which it is possible to reach the foot of the north-west ridge of the Huantsán in a single day.

Ticapampa, during the days preceding our departure, was the scene of feverish activity, with every member of the party busily engaged, preparing for the assault. We had no time to recuperate from the Pongos ascent. In any case we weren't in a mental state to think of resting or relaxing. We were now on top of our form—and every day lost might lessen our lead over the American expedition.

By way of taking time by the forelock, Blasido, now quite fit again, was sent on ahead by mule to the Chavin valley, charged with the hiring there of pack-animals. In this way we thought we could travel later to the other side of the range and then avoid being obliged to devote several days making such transport arrangements. De Booy gave Blasido detailed instructions. It was agreed that he should meet us on the evening of June 15th in the Chavin market-place, from where, early the following morning, we should set off again.

On returning to Ticapampa we hoped to find our friend Raymond Grière there—we had calculated on his arriving by that time. But a great disappointment awaited us. Among the post which had arrived in our absence lay a telegram from Grière greatly regretting that he could not join the party. Whilst training in France he had sustained an injury which had proved more serious than originally

75

thought. His doctor had forbidden him to take part in any kind of sport for some time. This was a real setback. It meant a serious weakening of our team. Grière was not only a first-class mountaineer, but also a climber with considerable knowledge of the Andes. The strength of our group was thus radically reduced for the great undertaking ahead. A group of four was small enough, to be sure; but attempting an assault on the Huantsán with a party of three was almost bravado. On the other hand, it would be rather humiliating to alter our plans and choose a lesser objective at this late stage. We decided, come what may, to see the thing through.

Grière's dropping out involved us in other difficulties. In view of his knowledge of the Spanish language we had rather relied on his taking over the organizing of the transport, giving instructions to porters, and so on. Of the three of us, only De Booy spoke Spanish to any degree. It meant that the handling of the native porters would fall largely on the shoulders of our youngest member. During the past few weeks I had picked up a certain amount of Spanish and could make myself understood so far as elementary camp activities and so on were concerned. But when a discussion ensued, I immediately got into deep waters and had to call in De Booy to interpret.

In spite of Terray's recent stay in the Argentine he had the greatest difficulty with the language. His knowledge of Spanish was confined to 'Muy bien, muy bien,' which is best translated by 'O.K.' or 'All right!' We were to hear these words continually during the remainder of the expedition.

In those days of hectic preparations I saw practically nothing of my companions. They were busy all day long in the storehouse, sorting out and dividing kit and high-altitude provisions for the coming four weeks in the mountains. Dozens of cases and canvas bags were to be taken along, and lists had to be made out of the contents of each, so that we could find anything we wanted with the least delay. I myself sat at my typewriter from early morning till

late at night, writing articles for Dutch papers, dealing with correspondence relative to the expedition, and, in between whiles, writing long letters home.

The engagement of porters raised some problems. In addition to Eugenio and Blasido, who now had some experience of snow and ice, we wanted to take along two other men. The first applicant for the job was Blasido's brother-in-law, Leucadio, who had already served us in the capacity of *arriero* during our Pongos venture. We asked Eugenio whether he, too, had a strong, energetic friend or relative who would like our sort of work. A few days later Eugenio arrived with a dark-hued fellow of twenty-one, short and stocky, with broad shoulders, who said he would like to make one of the party. Like most local Indians he had a phenomenally wide chest. Neither Leucadio nor this Guillermo had ever set foot on a mountain.

In ordinary life Guillermo was a carpenter and a tailor. He looked serious and as strong as an ox, so we decided to take him. At this early stage we little suspected that he was to turn out by far the best of the porters and remain with us to the very end. When I returned to Holland, De Booy took Guillermo with him to Bolivia to help in further geological surveys.

Just when we thought the porter problem had been nicely settled there came a hitch. The morning before our departure, Eugenio, despite his agreement, said he could not come. Some cattle belonging to his parents—for whom he was responsible—had disappeared from their grazing grounds and had to be tracked down. We were at our wits' ends. We simply had to have another porter without delay. The ingenious De Booy hit on a solution. He offered a reward of five *soles* to anyone producing a substitute for Eugenio within half an hour. Five minutes later Eugenio himself came to claim the money. He brought along a young fellow named Pelegrino, strongly Mongolian in features, but of the same robust physique as Guillermo. He was normally one of the employees in

77

the washing-beds at the silver mine. We vetted him thoroughly, realizing that we were taking a considerable risk, engaging him at a moment's notice like this, without knowing anything about him. We made it clear what was expected and what his duties would be. De Booy asked if he felt at all scared, but he confidently replied that it was precisely the element of danger in our venture that attracted him. In point of fact it turned out later that this Pelegrino was the most faint-hearted of all the bearers. He had entered our service purely because the money offered by us was a little more than his ordinary pay in the silver mine.

The morning of June 15th was devoted to handing out clothing, footwear and equipment to our new recruits. Each bearer received the following:

1 woollen undervest	1 pair of mountaineering boots
1 pair of long woollen pants	1 woollen scarf
2 thick khaki vests	1 woollen beret
1 pair of thick army trousers	1 pair of gaiters
1 thick khaki battledress	1 canvas storm helmet
1 anorak or wind-cheater	1 pair of sun-glasses
1 thick woollen sweater	1 down sleeping-bag
2 khaki shirts	1 rucksack
2 pairs of woollen socks	1 pair of crampons
1 pair of gloves	1 ice-axe

Each item, as received, was carefully entered in a book and the complete list was signed by each bearer, together with an undertaking to return everything once the expedition was back in Ticapampa. We had already been taught a sharp lesson in this respect, for it was only after engaging our fourth porter that we had suddenly remembered Eugenio's kit and the need to get it back. Too late! He had already departed for Huaraz, taking with him a thick woollen sweater, a scarf, and a pair of mountaineering boots. But De Booy, who had been responsible in Holland for obtaining

equipment for all the bearers, had done a fine job. Even though Eugenio had gone off with this and that, there was still more than enough gear for the rest.

It was amusing to see the metamorphosis in the porters when they arrayed themselves in their new clothes. Pelegrino, in particular. Previously a short stout peasant, he changed at the dress rehearsal into a Chinese soldier. Even Leucadio, usually so shabby and scruffy, now acquired a certain distinction. The change in their appearance affected the men themselves. They swaggered amongst the villagers who were swarming round the entrance to the store and having a good look at everything these queer foreigners or *gringos* were doing.

Up to the door, at three o'clock, came the lorry which was to take us over the 15,000-ft. high Cahuish pass to the Chavin village on the east side of the range. But prompt departure was out of the question. About an hour before, Lionel had suddenly thought that it might be a sound precautionary measure to sharpen the points on the crampons. We waited impatiently till four o'clock before he was finally finished. Then we left; but half an hour later we were back again in Ticapampa. In the commotion Terray's rolls of films had been left behind in the store. It was about half-past four when we finally succeeded in leaving Ticapampa and the Santa valley, and moved slowly up towards the pass.

Terray was very elated. He had been far too long in the valley for his liking and he was now full of the coming attempt on the Huantsán. He let his imagination run riot and began toying ambitiously with the idea—after successfully climbing the Huantsán—of finding a new route to the summit of the highest mountain in whole Peru: the Huascarán, situated to the north of the chain.

Whilst Terray was so gaily talking of the Huantsán, larding his flow now and then by roaring out some bawdy French soldiers' song, I noticed that De Booy had suddenly become still and tense.

The big event that lay ahead meant so much to him. He had always concentrated, far more than I had, on the mountaineering side of the expedition, and the ascent of the Huantsán had become almost an obsession. This was very obvious when he suddenly looked at me, and said, 'Now it all *really* starts!'

I, myself, regarded what lay ahead with mixed feelings. The successful climbing of the Pongos, the most difficult that I had ever achieved in my mountaineering career, had considerably boosted my self-confidence. All the same, I could not help wondering whether we were not a little too presumptuous in proposing to tackle the Huantsán. The drastic weakening of our strength by the falling-out of Raymond Grière weighed heavily on me; and, looking at our little party sitting side by side there, I sombrely thought that a group of three men was exceedingly small for an enterprise of such magnitude.

I glanced at the porters, sitting there somewhat awkwardly, and tried to imagine how each would react in an emergency. How far could we really count on them? One could tell nothing from their individual expressions. Guillermo and Pelegrino were undoubtedly as strong as bulls, but, against that, they were totally inexperienced. They would be able to carry burdens on easy ground, but what about the rest of it? Leucadio was willing, but spineless. We had already noticed that he seemed to be entirely under Blasido's thumb. The absent Blasido was tough and enterprising, but, as we found out on the Pongos, no good at high altitudes. We could not expect much from him. Clearly, we should have to rely entirely on ourselves at great heights and be prepared to face up to terrific physical strain. But why worry prematurely? All of us were in the pink of condition. After all, the mighty Huantsán was well worth a mighty effort.

The nearer we approached the high pass the more impressive became the scenery. The view across the Querococha lake, with the Pucaraju in the background, was exceptionally beautiful. We pro-

During the ascent of the Pongos; Terray passing the ice-covered rocks

The south face of the Pongos, climbed during the ascent

ceeded slowly up and over the pass, absorbing it all. Then followed an endless winding track down to Chavin some 5,000 feet below.

The driver tried to make up for lost time by driving the loaded lorry at break-neck speed down the narrow path and round hairpin bends, hewn from the mountain side. I did not dare look too often at the depths along which we were careering. It did not require much imagination to guess what would happen if a tyre burst, or anything else went wrong. Even Terray, who was inured to travel in mountainous country, and who himself has been known to scorch like one possessed, began to look thoughtful. On one occasion when we missed going over the brink by inches, he broke off singing to remark that present-day chauffeurs in South American countries were all really efficient because the bad ones had long ago been killed; a sort of 'survival of the fittest'.

It was quite dark when the lorry was stopped not far from Chavin by Blasido, holding up a lantern in the middle of the road. He told us that he had hired a dozen horses and mules. He had met us at this spot because the *best* way to the Huantsán massif diverged at this point, and, according to him, it would be a waste of time to go through Chavin itself. In a flood of rhetoric he did his best to convince us of all this. But we knew better. Unlike Blasido, we had at our disposal an excellent topographical chart of the area, on which it was clearly to be seen that the Carhuascancha valley—our obvious route—lay to the north of Chavin. We had carefully weighed all the alternatives before deciding on this particular route. And here was this self-opinionated Blasido, trying to mess up our plans! De Booy told him, without further ado, to follow us to Chavin with the pack-animals, so that next morning we could resume our journey at the earliest possible hour. Blasido tried his very utmost to get us to change our minds. Only when it was clear that he simply was *not* going to get his way, did he let the cat out of the bag. Some of the pack-animals he had hired from a friend were unlicensed and he did not therefore want to take them into Chavin

F   81

Top left: The police take our names and addresses. With expeditions one 'can never tell what they may get up to'. Top right: On the way to the base camp. Foals faithfully follow the mare. Bottom: In the market-place at Chavin, just before our departure for the Huantsán mountain

where there was a police station. Now we were getting to the bottom of things! The animals had no registration papers because they were not the lawful property of the *arriero*, but were, let us say, acquired. One had to get used to dealing with all sorts of queer customers.

Months later, when we visited Chavin again to do geological work, Guillermo, with whom we were then on more intimate footing, told us that in these parts horse-rustling was quite an everyday affair.

So there we were without mules. It was an intregal part of our carefully planned programme to go through Chavin and we were not to be put off our course to oblige some pothouse friend of our bearer. We gave Blasido a dressing-down for being so headstrong and for failing to carry out instructions to the letter. De Booy gave him stern orders to replace the animals that very evening and to meet us next morning before eight o'clock in the market-place at Chavin.

Then our lorry started off again down the steep road to Chavin. We finally reached the little place about 8.30 and unloaded our equipment and stores by the light of our torches in the market-place. We wanted to settle up with the driver, but had no small change. A good half-hour was spent in going from house to house before we managed to get change for a 500-soles note.

At the only hotel in Chavin there was no food to be had. An Indian lad took us through the dark village street in search of a place to eat. We found a decayed little café, where the proprietress said she would get us a meal. It was beef steak with fried eggs and potatoes —all prepared with terribly strong herbs, the so-called 'Aggi'. Starving, we fell to, but after a few mouthfuls our throats felt on fire. It took glasses and glasses of beer to wash down this highly spiced meal. As we sat there in the poor flickering light of the oil-lamp, heads came peering round the door. News of our arrival had gone like wild-fire round the village and a large proportion of the

inhabitants had gathered in front of the café, full of curiosity to see what we looked like.

To Indian eyes, we must have appeared strange beings. It had been so cold in the open lorry that we had put on our orange-coloured eiderdown jackets. These were clearly regarded by the villagers as the Dutch national costume. Around our table swarmed not only our landlady's offspring, but also all their young friends who contrived to slip in. One little child, who could hardly toddle, climbed up beside me and kept stroking the soft smooth nylon of my jacket. But not only children surrounded us; there were four dogs, two or three guinea-pigs, and at least one cat. Feeling a movement near me on the bench, I stretched out my hand to pat as I imagined, a dog, and touched an indignant fowl. Terray was still in fine fettle, and his rollicking songs never had a more enthralled audience of young and old. It was the gayest, oddest party, with everyone in good spirits—I shall never forget it.

Late that night, we returned to the market-place and crawled into our sleeping-bags. We intended spending the night beneath the stars, for what we had seen of Chavin's only hotel was not particularly inviting. By sleeping in the open we not only saved hotel expenses, but, more important, we could keep a watchful eye on our gear. Once we were disturbed by two drunken fellows who tried to persuade us to come indoors to sleep. That incident over, we settled down to an excellent night.

Awakening next morning, we stared around in astonishment. Although only half-past five and still fairly dark, a ring of villagers stood there, patiently waiting for us to get up and start our weird activities. Never before had they seen a spectacle like this. They overwhelmed our porters with questions, and eyed and discussed our gear with avid interest.

Many of those villagers were an appalling sight. In all my life I had never seen such a collection of abnormalities—children with hydro-

cephalus, men and women with goitres, deaf and dumb, semi-blind, hunchbacks, dwarfs, and idiots. It was a pitiful picture. Only in the last few years had the remote village of Chavin become accessible to motor transport. The incidence of inbreeding was apparently very high. It was poverty at its direst. Most of the population were clothed in rags. It was the exception to see anyone with a coat, jacket, or trousers that had not been patched again and again.

As we had rather dourly expected, Blasido did not turn up at the appointed time, and we were forced to spend the whole morning in Chavin. Terray accepted this as a matter of course. On one occasion in the Himalayas he had waited seven days for transport. But it was otherwise with De Booy, who was irritated beyond measure to think that his carefully prepared programme was now going to pot —all through Blasido's waywardness. This would be the last time we took that bright beauty with us, we decided. Whilst waiting, we tried to kill time by talking to the bystanders, although, after some hours, these dwindled to a group of small boys. De Booy, who never missed a chance to practise his Spanish, asked one smiling youngster: 'Why aren't you at school? It is ten o'clock! Are you on holiday?'

The little chap came closer.

'No, Señor,' he said a shade awkwardly, 'we aren't on holiday. We've no teacher to-day.'

'Where's your teacher then? Is he ill?'

'No, Señor, he isn't ill. He's . . . drunk!'

De Booy managed not to change his expression.

'Oh, he's drunk, is he!'

'Yes, Señor.'

'How often does that happen?'

'It doesn't happen often: only once or twice a month.'

'I suppose you think that fine, eh?'

'Oh, yes, indeed!' agreed the youngster, beaming all over his face.

This exchange naturally provoked general merriment, but it had its repercussions. When, four weeks later, we returned from the Huantsán and were waiting one morning in the Chavin market-place, De Booy spotted the same youngster amongst the crowd.

'Hello, don't you have to go to school to-day?' he exclaimed. 'Or is your teacher drunk again?'

This time the lad did not laugh, but only shook his head sheepishly. The grown-ups in the crowd laughed heartily, and pointed to a man who had been standing near De Booy, but who was now striding away, looking as black as thunder. It was the school-teacher! Someone, we surmised, would soon receive a good spanking.

But our talk was not entirely confined to youngsters. Now and then we were approached by adults, agog with curiosity to find out what we were up to. When we spoke of the Huantsán we realized with amazement that they simply did not know which mountain we meant. Although Chavin was situated at the end of the valley leading up to the Huantsán, hardly anyone in the village had ever seen the mountain at close quarters. One villager told us that Kinzl had lodged with him during the Professor's visit to this part of the range. We naturally tried to find out more. We should have liked to have discovered why the German attempt on the Huantsán had not originated from there: but nobody could throw any light on the matter.

The morning crept tediously by. We had almost given up hope of getting away that day. Then, about 12.30, Blasido rode into the square—like a prince at the head of a column of pack-animals. By way of welcome he got a blistering telling-off; I do not believe I saw De Booy in such a towering rage during the whole of our stay in Perú. Mustering all the Spanish at his command, he gave Blasido a piece of his mind in front of the entire population.

Then at top speed we set to work, loading our gear. There were nine pack-animals including various mules, one of which was par-

ticularly troublesome. Every time the *arriero* tried to load him he began to buck. Finally, after much struggling, the load was secured. But all at once the beast broke loose and set off at top speed down the road. He was quite a good distance away when, luckily, a passing Indian managed to catch him. All was ready at last for our departure.

Then a policeman suddenly came on the scene, asking us in a friendly manner for our names and addresses. He had heard of our plans. He would therefore like to be in a position to give the Dutch and French legations in Lima full details of any casualties. We were naturally helpful, but tried to make him understand that we did not exactly propose jumping off the top of the Huantsán. All his trouble might be in vain. The extremely courteous policeman did not altogether appreciate our type of humour. He hastened to justify himself. He was only acting from a high sense of duty. Eventually we went away with his best wishes and his heartfelt hope that he would not have to make use of our names and addresses.

The whole village turned out to stare as at half-past one we finally turned our backs on Chavin. At last we were on our way to the Huantsán. That day we moved northwards through the valley, a long monotonous journey. We went partly on foot and partly on horseback, finding the heat rather trying, although we were up some 11,000 feet.

When hiring animals we had fallen into the error of assuming that the owners would provide pack-saddles, but in the Cordillera Blanca this was apparently not always the case. Our cases and bags had mostly to be secured to our beasts by rope, and it became an all too frequent occurrence for our caravan to be halted because the load had slipped off a saddle-less mule. To the accompaniment of a torrent of rich Spanish expletives the ropes had to be untied and the load completely lashed up again. It was a delaying, temper-fraying process. We came through it all with a much extended vocabulary of ripe Spanish swear-words.

De Booy was still sore at Blasido who, as always, was having the most to say and handling his fellow-porters as though he were the cock of the walk. When, for some reason or other, another first-class row threatened, I was forced to intervene for the first and only time during the expedition and to use my position as senior member of the party in order to bring tempers down to a cooler level. Nothing is so menacing to the success of a mountaineering expedition as sour feeling at base camp, whether it be the result of bad relations between the members themselves, or between the climbers and their native bearers. We should really need our helpers during the coming critical weeks, and it was probable that they would be asked to give us of their best. A high degree of co-operation was only possible if our mutual relations were of the friendliest. Discontent could be fatal.

Towards dusk we reached the juncture with the Carhuascancha valley which would lead us next day to the mountain itself. We made camp here, near the last human settlement we were to see for some weeks. That evening we were too busy preparing for the night to make contact with the inhabitants, but early next morning De Booy, Terray and I went to have a look at the hamlet. We saw half-breeds in a state of the direst poverty, living under the most primitive conditions, and eking a miserable livelihood from a little agriculture and animal breeding. At first they were shy and suspicious, but when we gave the ragged children sweets their confidence was quickly won. They looked on smilingly whilst we took coloured films and photographs of the village.

Just as we were about to depart, a wizened old crone emerged from one of the houses with an egg in her hand. She offered it to us as a token of friendship. On seeing this, out came other women carrying eggs. We accepted these with a politeness which was obviously appreciated. Unfortunately, we did not have much time to spare. We wanted to reach the end of the Carhuascancha valley that day and to set up our base camp at the foot of the Huantsán.

The track through the valley led steeply up, through hewn-out walls, and we speedily began to notice the effects of the altitude. At many places the rock strata were covered with red-coloured plants, producing a particularly lovely effect. Time after time we stopped to take shots with our cameras. We were all eager to catch a first glimpse of our mountain, but unfortunately the clouds were hanging too low over the valley.

In the afternoon De Booy and Terray rode ahead to look for a suitable spot for base camp. I, myself, remained with the column to keep an eye on things and, when necessary, spur the *arrieros* to greater speed, for the pack-animals moved slow-paced over the marshy ground of the valley.

THE FALL

Fairly late in the afternoon of June 17th the column neared the end of the Carhuascancha valley. In front of us a vast glacier seemed to stretch right to the foot of the Huantsán massif. I sincerely hoped that this was not the only approach to the mountain, as the glacier, with its tangle of treacherous crevasses, did not look at all inviting, to say the least. Even from this distance below, it appeared a hazardous proposition for our inexperienced porters to tackle.

The valley curved to the left and then came to a gradual end at a fairly steep scree-covered slope. De Booy and Terray were far in front and they must have gone up this slope. So I gave the signal to follow on, at which immediate protests arose from the *arrieros*. The terrain was too difficult for their beasts, they declared, but I stood firm. It was essential to establish our base camp as high as possible. The protests and the violent gesticulations continued. Blasido, to my great annoyance, took the side of the *arrieros*. There was a brisk exchange of hard words before I finally got my way.

As Guillermo and I went ahead to find the simplest way, we sud-

denly saw De Booy high above us on the slope, waving his axe.
Half an hour later we reached him and heard that an ideal spot had
been found for the base camp on a level stretch at the side of a small
lake. Terray, it seemed, had gone still higher to reconnoitre the
approach route to the mountain.

An hour later the whole column came up. It began to drizzle, so
we hastened to pitch camp. The altimeter registered 14,450 feet.
There was little to be seen of our surroundings that afternoon: the
mountains were shrouded in cloud. The Huantsán, too, remained
invisible.

Not until dusk had fallen did Lionel return from his reconnaissance. He had first climbed up the northern tongue of the glacier, but
found that this did not offer a likely approach to the mountain. The
enormous crevasses seaming the surface would have made a serious
handicap even for skilled Alpinists. With inexpert porters, such as
ours, we should certainly land in overwhelming difficulties.

The more southerly tongue of the glacier seemed to offer better
possibilities. At that moment it looked as though it were flowing
down from the clouds to terminate a few hundred yards above our
camp. A fair portion of this, too, appeared impassible. But along its
left flank ran a narrow gully, which did not look too complicated,
though it certainly had one distinct drawback. For a distance of
several hundred yards it passed below an icefall which had the usual
chaos of giant *séracs*,[1] many of which were overhanging and looked
decided wobbly. Terray did not minimize the dangers. He told us
that the gully was strewn with blocks which had obviously crashed
down from above. Naturally he was not precisely enthusiastic
about taking this way, but, after carefully examining all other possible routes, was convinced there remained no alternative. To try to
reach the higher part of the glacier via the steep rocks bordering it,
was out of the question. They were far too slippery and heavily ice-

---

[1] *Seracs* are large angular or tower-shaped masses into which a glacier breaks up
at an ice-fall.

coated to afford sufficient holds. So if we did not wish to throw up the sponge at this early stage, there was nothing for it but to brave the perils of the gully with as cheerful a face as possible. To reduce the risk we agreed that it would be best to cut down to the minimum the number of journeys required to be made through this dangerous part of the ravine.

Meanwhile the rain had turned to sleet. In less than no time the newly-pitched tents had a half-inch coating of wet snow. It did not augur well. If this was our greeting from the Huantsán, it was obvious that we were not welcome.

The next morning our worries appeared to have been needless. It was beautiful weather. As usual Terray was up first, and he shouted to De Booy and me to come outside the tent. There, high above the glacier, rose our goal, the majestic Huantsán, an enormous fortress of ice and rock, thrusting into the heavens, its shape sharply etched against the clear blue sky. The three of us stood there, awestruck. Its height and breadth dominated the entire landscape. It was as though the mountain wanted to parade its colossal stature and to impress us mere insignificant men, proclaiming: 'Here am I, the mighty, unconquered Huantsán!'

To the left we saw the higher south summit, and to the right the long ridge ending in the north summit. The full run of this ridge was unfortunately not discernible, but it was clear that the mountain would have to be attacked from the north. Using large field-glasses we studied all the possibilities. The northerly ridge of the south summit looked difficult, but not entirely insuperable. Terray expressed concern about a possible cornice, which might then be hidden from view, because we were, so to speak, on the windward side of the massif.

To me, curiously enough, the mountain was now far less terrifying than I had anticipated. The photographs I had been looking at so intently in the past few months had tended to build up the impression that the Huantsán was an enormous unscalable pyramid with

fantastically steep walls and inaccessible ridges. Looking at the mountain from various angles on several occasions during our stay in the Cordillera Blanca had not lessened its formidable effect. But now, seen from this present point, its whole structure fell into easier perspective: my self-assurance soared.

Perhaps there was a psychological side to this. A difficult mountain invariably loses some of its more frightening aspects the closer one gets to it, the more one looks at it, and the more one thinks about it.

Our subconscious minds had been continually grappling with the route question. We had been mentally facing up to all sorts of contingencies. Anxiety now gradually gave place to the feeling that we were already half-way there. Hitherto I had never been under illusions about our chances of reaching the top. With the mountain right in front, all this now changed. There *was* a chance! This mountain was not unclimbable.

Terray, too, was in high spirits. Now we were so near our goal, he did not want to lose a single moment. We divided a large quantity of provisions between the rucksacks of three porters, and towards noon Terray and I set out with Pelegrino, Leucadio and Guillermo, to take up our first load via the tongue of the glacier, to the foot of the Huantsán. Crampons were donned when a point just below the icefall was reached, as it was essential to negotiate this dangerous part as quickly as possible. But our bearers were using crampons for the first time and did not find things easy. Terray had Pelegrino and Leucadio on the rope, and I had Guillermo. Some parts of the gully were fairly steep. Once, as I followed close behind Leucadio, he fell back, almost into my lap. I only just managed to avoid his spiked crampons.

It took a good fifteen minutes to get past the tottery séracs. At this height rapid climbing made exacting demands on lung capacity. Once we were through the danger zone we simply had to give ourselves a breather. But Terray gave us little respite, and we were all

anxious to find out how the route looked a little further up. For several hours we climbed the glacier, keeping up a good pace although its cover of snow was so soft that we sank knee-deep in many places.

Guillermo, who was following me, climbed as though he had never done anything else. His rucksack contained three times more weight than mine, yet I had a feeling that he was exerting himself far less. It was amazing to watch the instinctive ease with which he negotiated tricky parts and how he contrived to place his crampons in just the right way. He listened attentively to advice.

The weather gradually became worse. From where we were contouring nothing much could be seen of our mountain. Climbing a stiff snow-slope, we finally reached a spot some 17,000 feet up, at the base of the north-east face. Terray regarded the site as suitable for our first assault camp. We dug a deep hole in which we placed our loads. It had started snowing again, so we descended the glacier as quickly as possible and swiftly passed the icefall.

The next day De Booy took my place. In order to ferry as much material as possible up to Camp 1, they took Blasido with them as well this time. I was thankful to stay at base camp and get a little rest. And it *was* wonderfully restful, even if the silence was shattered every few minutes by the roar of avalanches or the crash of collapsing séracs. Something was always happening up there on the Huantsán. In the late afternoon a noise sounded so close at hand that I scrambled out into the open, full of apprehension. The party ought, by then, to have been near the icefall. I looked anxiously about. That last crash had seemed so ominous. Then, as I moved more into the open, I saw the porters already on the moraine. A few moments later Terray and De Booy came careering down the slope. They told me that while they had been resting for a moment near the glacier they had seen a block of ice 'calve off' from the tongue and fall with a resonant crash into the glacial lake.

De Booy was enthusiastic about Guillermo and Pelegrino. They

had acquitted themselves well on the ice, and had made the descent in little over an hour. Only once had the pace slackened and that was when Pelegrino had suddenly disappeared to his shoulders in a snow-covered crevasse.

On the next day, June 20th, the attack proper would begin. We decided to take the two strongest bearers, Guillermo and Pelegrino, to establish Camp 1. Blasido and Leucadio would remain at base camp.

Came the dawn! The weather was fine. We all felt optimistic about our chances of success. A good quantity of stores was already high up the mountain. Conditions generally were favourable. Our spirits soared as, setting out from base, we said cheerio to the rearguards.

There was no particular need to hurry, so we took things fairly leisurely and on the way up did some filming. Camp 1 was pitched that afternoon in its chosen place, close to the east face. From this point we gained a good view of the lower reaches of the Huantsán. We scanned the mountain meticulously, probing all the possibilities. Terray finally drew up a plan of attack. Our first objective would be to reach a small plateau about 19,000 feet up, situated directly below the north summit. There we would establish our second assault camp.

It would then be essential to get up adequate provisions with the minimum loss of time and energy. The jagged north ridge looked very forbidding, so Terray decided to avoid its lower parts and cut across the steep north-east face—an audacious plan, for the face looked difficult and the porters would not be able to accompany us. Consequently it would not be possible to take all the necessary stores up to Camp 2 in one trip. We should have to return, and then a day or two later renew the attack, this time for the final assault.

On June 21st De Booy and I woke early, only to find Terray already out and about, busily preparing breakfast. We wanted to get up and help him, but he told us to lie on, as cooking was definitely

a 'one-man job'. Needless to say, we gladly accepted this advice. It was bitterly cold at that height in the early hours. Moreover, those few quiet moments gave De Booy and me time to prepare ourselves mentally for whatever the day might bring. De Booy, as it happened, was not feeling absolutely fit. He was suffering from stomach trouble and needed medicine to put him right. Another half-hour and we left our sleeping-bags.

At 7.15 everything was ready. We roped up and departed, climbing quickly over the glacier towards the selected point from which we intended tackling the face. The weather held promise of a fine day. After an hour's progress we reached and crossed the bergschrund[1] without incident. A stiff ice-slope led up to the rock wall. Although faced with no very great difficulties, our speed was slowed down by shortness of breath. We went some hundreds of yards up the rocks. Then came a steep snow-covered ice-slope across which we would have to go to reach the higher parts of the north ridge.

It was now ten o'clock. De Booy and I pleaded for a few minutes' rest before beginning to negotiate this ice-slope, but Terray was adamant. He was concerned at the ice masses poised above us. In his opinion they did not look at all safe, but rather as if they might crash down at any moment. He granted us barely time to take a sip from our flasks and to munch a few dried fruits. A little later we were determinedly tackling the slope.

We estimated that the traverse would take about two hours, then, allowing another two hours for negotiating the ridge itself, we thought to reach our objective by two o'clock at the latest. We would then have four hours' daylight for the return journey. But things turned out differently. . . .

Dimensions in the Cordillera Blanca are very different from those in the Alps and could mislead even a man of Terray's ripe experi-

[1] *Bergschrund* is the crack or crevasse separating the upper reaches of a glacier from the mountain.

ence. Studying the wall from below, he had perhaps misjudged the perspective. The view had also given us the erroneous impression that the wall was less formidable than was actually the case. The fact remained that our plans went awry. There seemed to be no end to the traverse. The gradient was always round the 50-degree mark. The ice-pitch was covered with mushy snow which had a treacherous way of sliding from beneath our feet. Only with difficulty could we find footholds with our crampons.

The utmost care was necessary. To avoid the chance of any member of the party falling, we worked to a definite system. The axe was rammed as deeply as possible in the snow and then, with a turn of the rope, an anchorage was obtained. Terray, who was always climbing a rope's length ahead, would drive in his axe with the kletterhammer, and then secure me. When I reached him, I then belayed De Booy, whilst Terray went on another 100 feet. This manœuvre was repeated time after time. It naturally took time, but it had one decided advantage. Whilst waiting for one another we did get an opportunity to recover our breath. This was a real relief for me, as I seemed to be insufficiently acclimatized and the rarefied air made me very breathless.

It was difficult to judge how many rope-lengths we should need to traverse the wall. Quite apart from the technical difficulties and the exhausting toil our position on the wall was far from pleasant because of the constant menace of the poised masses of ice projecting from the ridge and the north summit. Every now and again fragments would break off and hurtle down with frightening velocity. We certainly counted ourselves lucky not to be hit. By one o'clock we had only negotiated half the wall. It was now clearer than ever that our attack had failed. As soon as we attained the ridge we should have to return, so as not to be caught by nightfall on the mountain.

Technical hazards did not permit of our taking a single risk, and it was almost another three tedious hours before we finally reached

the *arête*. No less than six hours had been devoted to the traverse—hours of fatiguing ice-work—gruelling hours which had taxed us to the limit, carrying, as we were, heavy rucksacks in the burning sun. When finally we stood on the crest at four o'clock, even the iron Terray was somewhat spent. He was not only tired, but anxious.

Only two hours of daylight were left, far too short to make a descent down the north ridge, an unpleasant undertaking at the best of times. Snow conditions were unfavourable, but there was no other course open to us. What we could see of the ridge was not very encouraging. It was plain that Terray, too, saw no easier way out of it. We were caught, more or less, like rats in a trap. De Booy and I wondered whether we should not be obliged to bivouac somewhere on the ridge. It was best in any case to try and get as low as possible.

We started down the *arête*, but new dilemmas again slowed down our speed. Enormous bulging cornices made sections of the ridge practically impassable, and the only protruding rocks were so weathered that they crumbled as pitons were driven in.

'Ah, c'est moche!' exclaimed Terray, obviously most uneasy about the turn of events. This was the only occasion during the whole Huantsán expedition when we saw him really nervous. Indeed, it required little imagination to appreciate the critical nature of our position. In one place it took Terray more than half an hour to hack away part of the cornice. It was punishing work, making heavy demands on his reserves. But not only the cornice, everything else seemed to combine to make it an extraordinarily precarious passage. At another point we had to worm our way on our stomachs down an almost perpendicular part of the ice-ridge.

We quickly realized that this descent via the ridge was going to take longer than the remaining daylight. When, about five o'clock, we reached some slightly more favourable rock formations Terray decided to try a last expedient—anything to spare us from spending

Top left: A giant cactus in the Chavin valley

Top right: Llamas

...tom: An Indian
...t made of loam
...d puna grass—
...the 13,500 feet
...el

the night on this exposed ridge. He intended roping down the west flank of the north ridge by a succession of rappels.

As usual, the moment he had made up his mind, he set to work. No hesitation. All uncertainty left him. Well secured by me, he descended a dozen yards or so to find a suitable place in the flank. He made skilful use of a miserable little crack in the rock to drive in a piton, on which to belay the rope. Fortunately we had two ropes, each 200 feet long. By tying these together, it was possible to descend a full rope length each time. Astride the ridge, De Booy and I, very tense, looked on whilst Terray prepared the rappel. Far, far below, our tent camp was just visible. Spotting our porters moving about, we called in chorus and waved our arms until at last they responded and waved back. The first piton was fixed, but still Terray was not satisfied. He had lately acquired a wholesome respect for my weight and was afraid that this piton might not hold me. Some time elapsed before a second piton was placed in position, and then at last we prepared to move. Terray was to go down first, secured by me, to see to the second rappel. In the meanwhile we had unroped ourselves so that we could join the lengths and run them through the piton. Precious time was lost doing this. Ropes have an exasperating habit of getting all tangled up at critical moments, and that happened now. Before we were able to unravel all the twisted knots and loops, ten valuable minutes had flown.

At long last, all was ready. A few curt final instructions, and Terray slid down. About 200 feet below, at the end of the rope, he cut out a broad step in the ice-wall. Then I followed—first over a bulge, then a short distance dangling through the air, and finally down the steep ice-pitch of which the lower portion of the flank consisted. By the time I arrived, Terray had already hammered in a long ice-piton for the next rappel. We waited side by side, with our faces to the wall, until De Booy could join us. He had a most ticklish job. Whilst Terray during his descent had been secured by

me at the end of the rope, and I, in turn, had been safeguarded by De Booy, the latter now had to lower himself down by the double rope unsecured. He naturally went to work with the utmost caution, particularly when tackling the first stage over the bulge.

Terray and I looked at each other. Up above, when it looked as though we were caught like rats in a trap, he had been definitely apprehensive. Now he was back again to true form. He grinned at me and said:

'What a game! Ever been up against anything like this, Kees? Who would have guessed, this morning . . . ?

I smiled back. His magnificent self-assurance was infectious. I no longer doubted that, under his skilful guidance, we should extricate ourselves from this ugly situation. Nevertheless, we were not happy about the next rappel. The steep ice-wall (about 60 degrees) on which we were poised, went down another 100 feet or so and then abruptly ended in a void. Apparently the wall overhung at that point, but how far it projected and what came underneath, were imponderables. We could only assume that it would be exceptionally steep. We were, we thought, about 300 feet above the glacier at the moment. But the foot of the wall was not visible.

To our great relief De Booy joined us safe and sound on our little artificial shelf. We could now restart roping down from the lower piton. But would the rope be long enough to reach over the bulging overhang and enable us to gain a foothold lower down? Again Lionel went first so that he could make preparations as quickly as possible for the succeeding stage. About 100 feet down, he reached the edge of the bulge and could see what lay below.

'Ça touche nettement!' he called up. This was great news, for visibility was fading fast and we had not a moment to spare. A second later he disappeared from view, whilst De Booy and I waited in suspense. Then a vague reverberating shout came from below. To us above, it was completely incomprehensible. The words were lost under the overhang. Yet it was essential for me to know what

awaited me down below, so I bellowed out to Terray that I could not catch what he was shouting. De Booy and I waited anxiously, debating what to do next. Then we felt the tension on the rope slacken, indicating that Terray had found a foothold somewhere and had released the rope. Once again several precious minutes were lost. Then, further hesitation being out of the question, I let myself down the rope as quickly as possible until I reached the edge of the overhang. Peering warily over, I saw Terray about 80 feet directly below, clinging to the rock face.

The situation was unpleasant. The overhang projected so far out that the whole of the next 80 feet down had to be descended through space. Never before had I been faced with such a manœuvre. Thank goodness I was being secured from above by my companion. There was not much time to dally. De Booy had asked me to give him a shout as to the position so I called out that the rappel went fairly deep and that everything seemed all right. Then cautiously turning over on my stomach, I let my legs dangle into nothing, slid over the edge, and in the failing light began to descend the thin rope. This swaying through space made an unforgettable impression on my mind. The upper crust of the overhang was fringed with enormous icicles, one of which broke off as I accidentally came in contact with it and went tinkling past me down into the void. It was eerie.

If it had not been for the pressing time factor this would have been a thrilling adventure; but, suspended there, I was all too conscious that the occasion was not just another interesting descent. It was grim reality. A desperate race against time.

Further down the wall receded sharply away. I lowered myself, feeling very much like a spider on its thread, until my foot touched the ice-wall below. What a relief! As always, after a long descent by rope, it was wonderful to find one's feet again. Actually I had quite a job to get a footing, for the flank on which I landed was pitched at a gradient of at least 65 degrees and I was almost at the end of the

rope. There was little scope for manœuvring. Luckily Terray came to my assistance and cut out a few steps for me. He himself had had the greatest difficulty in arriving safely. What was worse, he found himself suddenly hampered by stubborn cramp in the arm.

I simply could not manage to get any more favourable stance than one with holds for one foot and one hand. I waited quietly for the next move, hoping that it would not take too long. It was De Booy's turn to come down. As experience had shown that it was useless to call out from below, I untied myself and gave three hard tugs at the rope, that being the agreed signal for him to follow down. He understood, for immediately there was a movement in the rope. Two minutes later his dim shadow appeared above on the edge of the overhang. In the meantime darkness had descended apace. A last spark of light seemed to linger on the spot where De Booy stood, but below the bulge, where we were, everything was shrouded in dusk. We exchanged a few words. De Booy asked what the position was like, and I shouted to him to try and land as high up the slope as possible because the rope was too short to allow of much playing about for position. I implored him to take the utmost care. One end of the rope was longer than the other, I bawled, but he ought to be able to manage.

Like some dim ghost De Booy slid down the thin nylon rope. Everything was going so swimmingly that I jocularly complimented him on his style. But, as he tried to get a foothold on the ice just above me, the treacherous light misled him. The slope was far steeper than he thought. His feet slid away. His hands found no hold on the slippery rock, covered with verglas. The heavy weight of his rucksack pulled him down and over backwards, and . . .

He fell.

To my horror he fell past me. Several yards lower however, he was brought up with a jerk, hanging head downward, his feet tangled in the rope. I frantically concentrated on ways and means of rescuing him. My own delicate position prevented me from get-

Half-Indian (Mestizo)

ting nearer. The wall, where I was precariously poised, was terribly steep, and the rocks at my side were covered with ice. Somehow or other I managed to grasp the looped end of the longer rope which was hanging loosely down and gave it a turn round my hand. Then, by grabbing the other rope, I formed, as it were, a continuous ring of rope, from a part of which De Booy hung upside-down. This action, I thought, would at least reduce the possibility of his slipping away. My brain worked feverishly, taking in every detail, trying to straighten out things, wondering whether De Booy's hands were also still clinging to the rope. If his feet did not untangle, he might be able to hold out until Terray came to his aid. I saw the latter some ten yards to our right on the slope, busily unearthing his torch from his rucksack. It had all happened in a matter of seconds, and as yet he had noticed nothing amiss. Only when I lustily yelled for help did he realize what was up. Then, without even giving himself time to grasp his axe, he sped across the wall towards us. And once again my heart stood still! He, too, missed his footing.

Some forty feet or so further down he managed, in his own inimitable way, to save himself. Thank God! For a moment he was completely dazed: he had wrenched his arm. I cried out to him to do his utmost, for De Booy's life was in peril. He could not possibly hang on the rope much longer.

De Booy was aware of this, too, for he said in a remarkably quiet voice:

'This is it, Kees! It's all over with us.'

But I still had hope. I called out that it wasn't all over! He must do everything to hang on! Then I focused my attention again on Terray who, on my other side, was laboriously climbing up the steep slope. It was slow, agonizingly slow. I spurred him on: 'Quicker, Lionel, much quicker!'

Then I heard a rending noise. I turned instantly to the other side, only to see De Booy plunging down towards the glacier. For a

Our Huantsán base camp, up at 14,450 feet

dramatic second or two I followed his fall as his crampons scraped the rock and sent up showers of sparks. Then he vanished in the void. A terrible silence followed.

Terray and I clung, petrified, to the face. Black despair for our comrade choked us. I saw no reason to call out. De Booy could hardly have escaped being killed.

Staring into the darkness below, I thought I could distinguish a vague dark blob against the white snow. From his greater distance Lionel had secured a rather better view. He had the feeling that, if De Booy had not bashed his head against projecting rocks and had avoided falling into the bergschrund, he might possibly be alive. He called at the top of his voice: 'Tom! Tom!' The dead silence seemed to confirm our worst fears; but Terray kept on calling and suddenly there came an answer—an unmistakable answer!

What a wonderful moment that was! To hear a voice, as it were, from the dead! For a time we were almost too astounded to react. Then we realized that the incredible had happened. An excited babble of Dutch and French went up. Anxiously we yelled to ask what he had broken. From the depths came the laconic reply: 'Nothing!'

A few moments later we saw a tiny light appear some hundreds of feet below. We had brought out with us special 'forehead' lamps in case we ever had to climb in the dark. The light was fastened on an elastic band which went round the forehead, thus enabling one to have the hands free. De Booy had obviously put his on to show us where he was. Seeing his light was our signal to get into action. Terray climbed up towards me and pulled at the end of the rope, but it wouldn't budge. This was the worst that could possibly happen at such a critical time. The nightmare thought of a jammed rope after a rappel over an overhang is always enough to give any climber grey hairs. Terray pulled with increasing force. He raged and swore—and, curiously enough, it seemed as though this helped, for suddenly the rope freed itself and was easily pulled

through. Terray worked with might and main to prepare a new rappel. Once it had been rigged up, I was able to leave my awkward position and slide downwards, feeling my way in the dark. The rope reached to about 65 feet above the bergschrund. I cut a big step with my axe and then waited for Terray to join me.

Meanwhile I could talk more easily with De Booy. My disquiet lessened considerably when he called out: 'Why the devil are you two taking so long? I showed you the quick way down, didn't I?' This was an encouraging sign. That he could still wise-crack cheered me up no end. I saw his light going to and fro and assumed that he was moving about to keep warm. He even climbed a little way up the slope to give me some light when, a little later, I came, via the bergschrund, on to the glacier. Terray followed closely behind. The three of us stood united again at the foot of the slope.

In the dark it was naturally impossible to trace the line of De Booy's fall. Not until next day were we able to assess its length and direction. But even in the dark one could tell that he had fallen at least 300 feet. He had been hanging upside down when he started falling and must have turned a somersault. His feet had struck the rock face some yards lower down and had taken the first brunt of his fall.

This probably saved his life. The steep ice-wall down which he had slithered with ever-increasing velocity was actually fraught with much less danger. We reckoned that he cleared the gaping mouth of the bergschrund which, at this point, was several yards wide, by sailing right over it. Landing on the sloping glacier, he had gradually lost speed because it was thickly covered with snow.

At that time all this did not interest us so much as finding out if he really were uninjured. It was almost unbelievable. He was examined in the light of our torches and prodded all over. A first glance only revealed a skinned nose. He complained of pains in the back. How could it be otherwise after a fall of some 300 feet? He was also

chilled to the marrow, a poor condition to be in with the prospect of an ice-cold bivouac at a height of 18,000 feet without tent or sleeping-bag. It was clear now that we should have to spend the night on the glacier, for De Booy was in no fit state to cope with a descent lasting several hours.

As soon as we found a more or less suitable spot we levelled it off as far as possible and laid down the ropes to insulate us a little from the rising glacial cold and to keep us as dry as possible. We then put on everything that we could find in the shape of clothing. We took off our boots and put on dry socks. Then we got into our nylon bivouac-sets, consisting of a long anorak and a narrow bag in which to place the legs, the so-called *pied d'éléphant*. Both parts fastened together with press studs.

We also drew our rucksacks over our feet to help keep them warm, and thus installed ourselves for the night. For extra security we belayed ourselves with ropes attached by a turn or two to axes rammed in the ice—a necessary precaution, as several yards away down the slope an enormous crevasse gaped open and we had no desire to slide into this in our sleep.

Actually we hardly snatched any sleep. The air was crystal clear and the pitiless cold cut us to the bone. Terray and I had De Booy between us, and were continually rubbing and massaging him, but we found it difficult to keep him at all warm. We, ourselves, had to keep on piano-playing with our fingers and toes. Blood circulation had to be maintained at all costs to prevent frost bite. If we dozed off, it was only to wake a moment later, disturbed by some movement of the others or tormented by the terrible thirst from which we now all suffered.

I unearthed a lemon from my rucksack and squeezed some of its juice on lumps of sugar, which I tried to get to De Booy. But it was no good. The acid lemon-juice caused him acute agony, owing to split lips. Then I tried to obtain some water to drink by filling my field-flask with snow and putting it under my clothes against the

bare flesh. Apparently I, too, must have been near freezing-point, because the snow did not melt.

There is no comparison between a bivouac in the Cordillera Blanca and one in the Alps. In Europe a bivouac lasts only about seven hours and one can get going again towards four in the morning. In the Andes it gets dark about six and the night lasts a full twelve hours. Even when dawn breaks, no start is possible because it is still too freezingly cold and the risk of frost-bite is too great.

It seemed that the wretched night would never end. We tried to divert our thoughts. Amongst other titbits, Terray told us of the many bivouacs he had endured in his career. He spoke of that terrible night on the Annapurna when, at an altitude of 23,000 feet, he had huddled in a crevasse with his companions, two of whom, Lachenal and Herzog, were suffering horribly from frost-bitten extremities. His last bivouac had occurred the previous winter on the vertical face of the Fitz Roy in Patagonia.

None of us had much heart for talk. Our thoughts were too taken up by our recent nerve-racking experiences and by the miraculous turn of events. What would have happened if De Booy had broken an arm or a leg? He could not possibly have survived this bleak icy bivouac. Yet there he was between us, apparently unscathed. We wondered if and when we should ever be able to renew the attack.

Thinking of the past eventful hours, I realized that it was not only De Booy who had enjoyed fantastic luck. Terray, too, might have hurtled precipitously down that face. And, if both of them had been seriously injured, what chance should I have had, without a light, to grope my way down that wall in the dark? Yes, we were all lucky to be still alive and kicking.

De Booy told me much later of his own sensations during that fateful fall and how he had reacted psychologically. This is his story in his own words:

DE BOOY'S OWN ACCOUNT

When I eventually reached the edge of the bulge it was getting dark. Looking down, I could see little more than the shadowy shapes of Egeler and Terray on the slope far below. At first sight, the pitch on which I had to alight did not appear excessively steep. Egeler called out to me to try and land as high as possible as the rope was too short to enable me to reach a more suitable place lower down the slope. Feeling very much the spider on the thread, I let myself down the thin nylon rope into the depths until at length my feet touched the slippery ice-face. Then, to my horror, I suddenly realized that it was far steeper than I had imagined. In the failing light I had sadly underestimated the pitch. As I slithered, I felt the heavy weight of my rucksack pulling me backwards. I frantically tried to get a grip on the rocks directly to my right, but they were covered with ice and offered no hold whatsoever.   *I fell.*

By some miracle I was pulled up with a jerk several yards lower down, my feet having somehow caught in the lower end of one of the double ropes. I dangled head down over the abyss, not daring to make a single movement. Only my companions could now save me from hurtling into the depths. I myself was helpless.

Egeler was himself perched in far too awkward a position to assist. Nevertheless, he tried to catch hold of my rope, and shouted loudly to Terray for help. My last hopes rested on Lionel. But in his haste to speed across to help me, he forgot to bring his axe; and he, too, slipped. Luckily, in some adept way, he just managed to check his fall some fifteen yards or so lower down. This, of course, I could not see. All I heard was an agonized French oath, then a panting voice urging me to have patience for another five minutes. It was then, at that precise moment, that I fully realized that as soon as my feet and the rope parted company, I would irrevocably plunge into

the void. It was a strange sensation, to become conscious that I was going to die. Oddly enough, I felt calm and untroubled by pangs of fear. Death seemed so inevitable that I simply accepted my lot. Thus it was that, suspended head downwards, I was able to remark to Egeler: 'This is it, Kees! It's all over with us!'

If there had been the slightest chance of surviving, I should no doubt have been terribly scared. But I felt no apprehension; only a feeling of relief, coupled with curiosity as to what death would be like. These thoughts were still flitting through my mind when I suddenly felt the rope leave my feet, and I dropped into space. What now? Death! A shower of sparks flashed in the darkness, convincing me that the end had come. It never occurred to me that they could have been caused by my crampons scraping the rock-face. I was hazily conscious only of sparks and a severe jolt in the back. I waited for the finish, but, to my utter amazement, I became aware that I was sliding through the crisp snow on the glacier. I had 'landed safely'. As soon as I could, I scrambled to my feet. Slowly it dawned on me that I not only lived, but that, by some providential means, I had not even broken a limb. It was almost too much to take in; so I was slow to reply to Lionel's shouts from high up the wall. At last I found my voice and yelled back: 'Ça va! Je n'ai rien du tout.'

I still felt as if I were in a dream. It seemed so incredible to be still alive, when I had already given up all hope of survival. I remember, as I opened my eyes, seeing the Southern Cross, that constellation of stars which is always such an attractive feature of the night sky in the southern hemisphere. It was one of the richest moments of my life. Standing there on the glacier, after falling some 300 feet, I was overwhelmed by the drama of this moment.

But my stupor did not last long, for the piercing night cold brought me shiveringly back to earth. It became imperative to do something to keep myself warm. I was intrigued to notice that my rucksack had remained in place during the fall, and that my sun-

glasses, which I had pushed up on to my forehead, were still intact. The only things missing were my axe and the woollen scarf which I had wound several times round my neck just before the fall. Without a moment's further delay I put on all the clothing I could find in the rucksack. Then I waited patiently for Egeler and Terray.

RETURN TO BASE

We heard all this, of course, much later. That night, on the glacier, we were far too cold, too exhausted, and too tormented with thirst to pay much attention to any story. When at long, long last, about six o'clock, the first rays of dawn tinged the high peaks, we sighed with relief to know that there was indeed an end to everything—even to this dreadful night.

It now became possible to take a good look around. We had viewed the same scene the day before from the ridge, but then our situation had been so grim that there had been no time to take things in. We found ourselves that morning on a vast snow-covered glacier. All around us towered numbers of gigantic peaks. In front was the fantastically steep face of the Ranrapalca; the pyramidical Chinchey; and the razor-edged ridge of the Cayesh. In the distance we could even distinguish the Huascaran massif. Dawn slowly breaking over this splendid mountain world was a revelation, although at that time we were too frozen to appreciate all its exquisite beauty.

Curiously enough, now that the sun was not so far away it seemed, if anything, to have grown colder. The rays of the sun took exasperatingly long to reach our bivouac—not in fact until nine o'clock, and even then we boggled at the thought of making a start. It was necessary for us to spend several hours warming our benumbed limbs in the beneficial rays of the sun. It was going to be difficult to get over the miseries of the past night.

The Nevado Huantsán (20,981 feet). Photo taken from the air by Dr. H. J. Spann

We could tell how terribly cold it had been by the state of our nylon outer garments. Even the inner linings had a thin layer of ice. Our climbing boots were frozen solid. We tried as best we could to thaw them out before pulling them over our chilled feet.

Now the worst was over, reaction set in. I felt terribly lethargic. Diffidently, I asked Terray how things were with him, and what he said then made a deep impression on me, coming as it did from a mountaineer regarded as one of France's strongest athletes.

'I can hardly keep upright.'

This might have been an overstatement, but it made me feel a lot better. If Terray felt so spent, then there was no reason for me to be so crestfallen about my own lassitude. Both physical and mental strain had taken their toll, the latter perhaps in the greater measure. And they had also left their mark on the outwardly insouciant Terray. It was, for us, another proof of his very deep sense of personal responsibility as leader of the team.

Needless to say, De Booy was in the worst plight. Lolling in the sunshine, we did not notice much amiss in his appearance. I eyed him as he sat there, quietly chatting to us. It was amazing how anyone could manage to survive a fall of some 300 feet and a subsequent bivouac without showing greater signs of reaction. But, on the return journey, it soon became clear that this appearance had been somewhat deceptive. The first part of the descent went fairly well, but as we later made our way through deep snow, we saw that De Booy found it terribly hard going. Every five minutes or so he would ask us to stop and rest, and each time we could only get him moving again with the greatest difficulty. Then he would struggle doggedly on. In this way, after an hour or so, we managed to reach the lower section of the north ridge.

In expert style and without a single miscalculation Lionel found a path across the deeply-crevassed glacier. We were now close to a narrow pass or col down which the route to the more easterly situated glacier looked fairly simple. Before starting, we went up

Top: Terray leads two heavily laden bearers up the glacier. *Bottom:* The ice-fall below which our route lay, constantly threatened by overhanging séracs

the steep slope to the crest of the ridge. We wanted to try and attract the attention of the porters in the camp below, to let them know that everything was all right. They would be terribly concerned, we thought, at our failure to return the night before, as planned.

From the crest we saw the tents on the glacier-slope far below, but no sign of life. We raised a mighty shout in unison, hoping they would hear. Then we set off, intent on making the rest of the descent as quickly as possible. Going through the col, we saw that, by going down a steep slope, we could reach the other glacier without much difficulty. We were thankful for this small mercy. After the previous day's events any difficult descent *en rappel* would have been the last straw for De Booy.

I was indeed becoming seriously concerned about De Booy. He was plodding manfully on and on through the deep snow with really admirable tenacity, and doing his utmost to keep up with Terray and me. Although we naturally moderated our pace a great deal in those circumstances, it was obvious that he was nearly at the end of his tether. If only we could get to Camp 1! It would not, of course, be possible in his present condition to make the further descent to base camp, where we could have made him much more comfortable.

For over an hour we went at snail's pace down the snow-covered slope until De Booy gasped that he could go no further. As we were so close to the camp, we implored him to make one last effort. Once again he mustered up all his strength and managed by sheer grit the last slope. Then, absolutely all in, he fell headlong between the tents.

The ordeal was over. We were back once more amongst living beings. Camp 1, primitive though it was, could provide the creature comforts we craved: hot drinks, warm food, the shelter of tents and sleeping-bags; and above all the services of men who were not, like ourselves, utterly exhausted and tired out. Another fifteen minutes

saw De Booy attentively tucked in his sleeping-bag, dosed with aspirins and imbibing hot tea and lemon.

One of the first things we asked Guillermo was what Pelegrino and he had thought had happened when we did not return to camp the previous night. We were curious to know if they had been anxious. Then it came to light how little these fellows comprehended the real nature of our enterprise; and how woefully limited their knowledge of their own district. Guillermo replied: 'Oh no, we weren't worried at all! We saw you up there on the ridge waving to us just before nightfall. Pelegrino reckoned you had found a house somewhere on the other side of the mountain.'

Such abysmal ignorance left us flabbergasted. Not for a single moment had they pictured us spending the night in the open, without tent or sleeping-bag. Even when we told them what had happened, their reactions were no greater than if it had been a stroll down the village street. They simply could not appreciate what we had endured. Pelegrino, in fact, started making a song and dance about his own sufferings, complaining of headaches and biliousness. Three or four times that afternoon he asked when we were going back to base camp. He hardly vouchsafed poor De Booy a glance.

Guillermo, too, had apparently not been feeling too happy at that great height. Close to the camp he had carved in the snow *Dios es Amor* (God is Love) in enormous letters. The action spoke volumes in itself.

Descent to a lower level was out of the question for the time being. De Booy was very groggy, and it was necessary to keep a close watch on his condition. He lay there all that afternoon, staring out with lack-lustre eyes. We had hoped he would sink into healing sleep—but no.

I was worried to death, not knowing what to do for the best. I finally decided to take his temperature once more and was relieved to find that it was only 100° F. Terray and I held a brief consultation. As laymen our diagnosis was 'shock'. We did not think there

were any serious internal injuries, otherwise the reactions would have been different. To tell the truth, our medical knowledge was extremely limited, and we could only hope that we had not over-looked any important symptom.

As night fell I went in the tent to sleep beside De Booy. Although tired right out myself, I lay awake for a long time listening to his uneven breathing. A thousand thoughts went through my mind. What should we do if something were seriously wrong with him? How about the rest of the expedition? Futile to think of climbing the Huantsán: it was no mountain for only two to tackle. What worried me more than anything else, more than even the Huantsán, was the geological exploration still to be done. Could I possibly manage on my own? It was rather dubious. I could in any case only try and clear up the work as far as possible. What should we do if De Booy's condition deteriorated next day? How could we get him down the ice-fall? How many days would it take to reach the near-est doctor? All these questions tormented me before I finally got to sleep. Blessed oblivion!

Next morning I was brought back to wakefulness by Guillermo. 'Señor Doctor, aquí avena con thé.'' (Señor Doctor, here's your tea and porridge!) De Booy was awake, too. At first sight there ap-peared little improvement, a fact confirmed by his temperature. He complained again of severe pains in the back, but I hesitated to do more than massage him gently.

Lionel was also concerned about De Booy, but his thoughts kept turning to the mountain. When I went into his tent later that morn-ing to discuss the situation, he gave me his plans for that afternoon. He intended taking Guillermo and Pelegrino, with a quantity of provisions, up to a point near where we had bivouacked. He wanted to take photographs at the same time of the north-east face, the north ridge, and of the place where De Booy had fallen. Terray was obviously feeling in fine fettle again.

It struck me as an excellent idea, if only because it gave Pele-

grino something to do. He had harped on about wanting to go down, so it was with some amusement that I saw him carrying a heavy rucksack and setting off for the higher regions that afternoon, instead of going down to the base camp.

Terray and the porters managed to get back within four hours. When I congratulated Lionel on this fine bit of work, he surprised me by saying that he himself had had difficulty in keeping up with the more heavily-laden Guillermo.

De Booy's state that night once more left much to be desired. His breathing was stertorous and I had the greatest difficulty in getting off to sleep. I was awakened several times during the night. Then at last, to my great relief, I noticed his breathing gradually becoming more regular. Towards morning he fell into a deep, restful sleep, and I had the impression that the crisis was over.

He awoke late in the morning, feeling very much better, and said he himself had no objection to making the trip down to base that day, provided we fixed him up first with a stimulant. Base camp had many advantages, one highly important merit naturally being that it was 2,300 feet lower. We decided to go down during the course of the day, making it a leisurely trip.

De Booy now showed encouraging signs, too, of renewed appetite. Thirty minutes before departure we gave him a coffadyn pill, which worked wonders. Within a few minutes of taking it, he was his old active self again, wanting to help with the packing—so full of beans, in fact, that we warned him to take things more quietly, otherwise the effects of the pill would wear off too quickly.

At last we started the trek back to base. Although in the pink of condition myself, I had a job keeping up with De Booy. That was the best sign yet that he was well on the mend. A few days of complete rest, away from the tiring glare of the snow, good food, deep sleep, and then . . . Yes, we could then give serious consideration to a second attack on the mountain!

Making our way down the glacier, we reached the ice-fall only

to find that it had undergone a complete change in appearance. The largest of the freakishly-shaped séracs, one which had earlier given us many anxious moments when skirting by, had disappeared entirely. All that remained of it was a number of huge ice-blocks strewn in the gully, right across the route we had taken so many times. We passed through this dangerous stretch at top pace. Half an hour later we were back at base camp.

The first attack on the Huantsán lay behind. It had resulted in failure, but we were thankful that things had not been worse and considered that, taken by and large, the mountain had really dealt mildly with our first assault. But was the rebuff meant to be definite? Had we to take it as a warning to keep off, or else. . . . As a sign to pack up and keep going, while the going was good? To admit that we were licked?

None of us could stomach this. As Terray frequently said: 'Nous vaincrons, parce que nous sommes les plus forts!' This became our expeditionary slogan in the battle with the Huantsán.

THE BLIZZARD

It would have been difficult to have found a better place in which to convalesce than our base camp in the Carhuascancha valley. It was idyllically situated on the edge of a little lake which mirrored the surrounding mountains beautifully in its quiet water. The first few days after our return were spent in complete rest. We sternly forbade De Booy to do anything unless he really felt equal to it, and for once our warning was heeded. Terray and I busied ourselves photographing the surroundings. On one occasion Terray went up alone to the heights to do some filming.

Once he talked big about going for a swim in our enchanting little lake, and when we kept chaffing him, he felt obliged to keep his word. Full of expectation we watched him dive into the icy-

cold water, but—*brrrr!* Never in my life have I seen anyone nip out so fast as Lionel did on that occasion.

One morning we were awakened very early by shouts from the porters. They said a large deer had approached to within twenty yards of the camp. It was as big as a mule, they declared excitedly. Blasido had gone after it with his muzzle-loader.

Those were lovely, unforgettable days, and yet we could not tear our thoughts away from the mountain. Our first attempt had been a complete failure, but our determination to succeed seemed, if anything, to have grown. Little remained, however, of our earlier easy optimism. For me the Huantsán had become very much steeper and infinitely more lofty. At last I saw the mountain in its true proportions: a vast fortress of snow and ice, bearing no comparison whatsoever with the 13,000 footers in the Alps.

We realized, too, that this was going to be no quick, flashy conquest. Only by drawing up a carefully thought-out plan of attack, plotting our movements from day to day, was there any chance of reaching the top. Our experiences during that first attempt had convinced us that the north-east face offered no practicable route to the summit of the Huantsán. Not only was the face longer than anticipated, but its inherent dangers could not be ignored. The huge overhanging ice-masses fringing both the north ridge and the flank of the north summit constituted too great a risk. We had managed to worm safely past them once, but it would be tempting providence to try it again.

Neither did the north ridge offer much prospect. Our experiences on its lower portion certainly did not make us eager to set foot on it again. Along practically its whole length ran a dangerous cornice and, as we had noticed at the time, its higher sections were just as unprepossessing.

We simply had to find another way. Luckily there was one bright spot. The morning after the bivouac had given us ample time to study the mountain at close quarters from the north. It

struck us then that a ridge which ran in a north-westerly direction to a point not far below the north summit appeared less menacing than the north ridge. Its flanks admittedly were extremely steep, but the gradient of the *arête* itself, particularly in its lower reaches, was not too bad. And whole stretches seemed quite free of cornice. This looked the best possibility and none of us had the slightest hesitation in deciding on it.

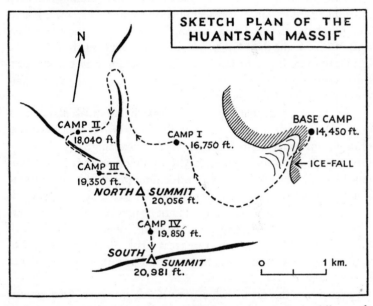

Sketch plan of the Huantsán massif, showing base-camp, ice-fall, assault camps 1–4, and north and south summits.

Lionel proposed the following assault plan. As soon as De Booy was fit and keen, we would leave the base camp for Camp 1. The following day we would establish Camp 2 a few hundred yards past the place where we had bivouacked. On the third day we

Camp 1 at 16,750 feet with the Nevado Cayesh visible in the background to the right

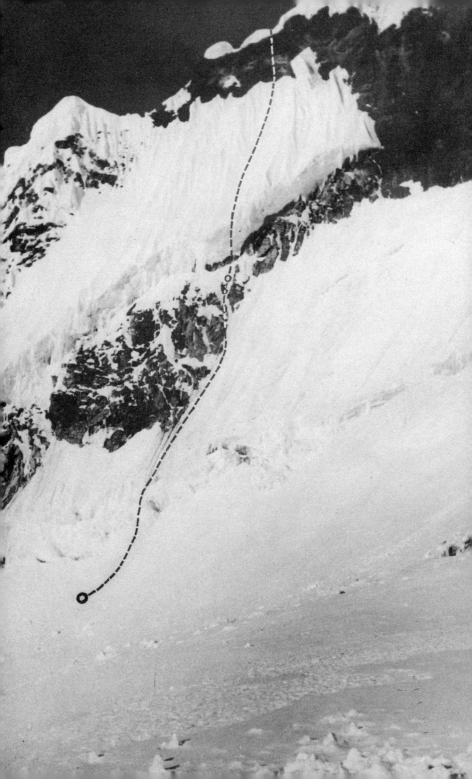

would try to force our way up the north-west ridge and establish Camp 3 as close as possible to the north summit. We would be obliged to carry very heavy rucksacks over long distances. Everything depended on whether, so weighed down, we could cope with that *arête*.

From below, the way from the upper end of the north-west ridge to the north summit looked fairly simple. Immediately after, however, came a section which posed a big query. Would it be possible to find a way down from the north summit to the saddle at the foot of the south summit? And, if so, would we be able to climb it again on our return journey? If not, then the descent would not be justified and another Huantsán attempt would have failed. We could only hope that we should be able to reach the saddle and establish Camp 4 there, so that, the following day, we could make our final all-out attack on the higher south summit.

Once the scheme had been drawn up, our self-assurance gradually returned. There seemed a good chance of success, and an important factor was that the distances set up to be covered each day were short. We felt in tip-top condition; we were acclimatized to the rarefied air; and we had the feeling that only bad weather could now rob us of success.

After six days De Booy had completely shaken off the effects of the fall. Not only had the stiffness gone from his loins, but—this was far more important—he felt right on top of the world and simply longed to have another go at the mountain.

The weather on the morning of June 27th left nothing to be desired. Accompanied by Guillermo and Pelegrino, we took our time going up the glacier towards Camp 1. De Booy wanted to spare himself as much as possible, so we took things very easily. It was past midday before we reached the camp and started putting things in order. Filming took up the rest of the day. After the evening meal, we crept into our sleeping-bags early in order to store up as much energy as possible for the strenuous days ahead.

The west flank of the Huantsán north ridge, down which we descended in the dark. The circles indicate the length of De Booy's fall

Next day, to our disappointment, the weather appeared to have changed. The cloud ceiling hung low over the mountains. The Huantsán was completely blotted out and mists repeatedly enveloped the camp. The wind, too, had increased in force. Nevertheless, we did not regard this as sufficient reason to postpone our attempt. We set off about ten, and made our way through the narrow col at the foot of the north ridge towards the northerly glacier. It was in this col that we met for the first time the full force of the wind. It did not augur well for the following day. And yet the fierce wind had one merit: it tore the mist to shreds so that large portions of the Huantsán kept coming into view.

After several hours we reached the site selected for Camp 2, to which Terray and the two bearers had previously brought up a considerable quantity of provisions. Whilst De Booy and I busied ourselves pitching the three two-man tents, Lionel went off to reconnoitre. He wanted to have a closer look at that north-west ridge. We saw him make his methodic way up the precipitous flank of the ridge with the easy, rhythmic movement of the first-class mountaineer, until he disappeared from view behind the snowy crest. The camp was almost completely organized when he returned an hour later. He told us that the proposed route was difficult, but, so far as he had been able to see, not insuperable. This was excellent news and put us in an optimistic frame of mind. The weather, too, appeared to be taking a turn for the better. The mists continued to hang low over the valleys, but were dispersing in many places on the higher ridges and we could see the clear blue sky above.

But once again things turned out contrary to expectation. About eight o'clock, before we could get to sleep, the first fierce gusts of wind came battering at the camp. At first we were not too worried, but as the frequency and force of the wind impacts increased, it became obvious that we were faced with a complete change in the weather.

This was most exceptional during the favourable season in the

Cordillera Blanca. The 'Wettersturz' so common in the Alps, where it is always a factor to be considered, is seldom encountered in the Andes. But on this Huantsán it seemed as though we were dogged by bad luck.

Towards midnight the wind had reached gale strength and was accompanied by storms of hail and snow. Some of the blasts were so strong that we began to wonder how long our small tents would resist the pressure. We had an uneasy feeling that there was a distinct possibility of our being swept, with tents and all their contents, into the depths below. At each shrieking blast we held on to the tent poles with both hands, buttressing them as much as we possibly could against the repeated sickening blows.

The drumming of the canvas, added to the howling of the gale, was deafening. Our camp stood close to the north face of the Huantsán and was thus exposed to the full fury of any tempest coming, like this, from a northerly direction. Then, on top of the constant thrashing of canvas, came the slapping rush of snow as it was swept against the windward side of the tent. Sleep was quite out of the question in this hellish maelstrom. We could only wait for the break of day.

But dawn brought no relief. The camp was shrouded in thick mist, the blizzard had buried us under deep drifts of snow, and there was no indication whatever of the storm diminishing in severity. On the contrary, it seemed worse. With reckless courage, De Booy crept outside to take a look at things, but came back a minute later with the news that conditions outside were impossible. The force of the wind was so terrific that one could scarcely stand or breathe. De Booy could not slip back quickly enough into his sleeping-bag. During the few moments he had been outside his whole being had become numbed. His hands and feet were dead with cold. We thought back to the bivouac of the previous week. Had we then been overtaken by such a storm as this we should have inevitably perished on the glacier.

Towards midday Terray fought his way across to our tent. As sole occupant of a two-man tent he had automatically assumed responsibility for the cooking, and he now brought us and the porters some porridge and Milo malt drinks. Lionel jeered at our concern about the storm, and said it was nothing in comparison with the fearful hurricanes he had experienced in Patagonia during the Fitz Roy expedition. He estimated the gale force at only 55 m.p.h.

Then he came out with the unwelcome announcement that we should have to turn out to put things in order. Many articles, such as crampons and cooking utensils, had been carelessly left outside the previous evening and were now buried deep in the snow. They would be lost for ever unless we jumped to it. It was a wretched job, demanding much time and energy. When at length we were able to get back to the shelter of the tent, it appeared that all sorts of items were still missing. My crampons were nowhere to be found, and, even more important at the moment, a leather field-flask, filled with alcohol for cooking purposes, had also vanished. Not being able to obtain any spirit supplies in the Santa valley, we had to have recourse to ordinary alcohol (40 per cent) for cooking. It was the sort the Indians used to drink. We found that it also 'lit up' our stoves quite well.

In the tents conditions were gradually becoming more and more unpleasant. Powdery snow was being driven by the wind through the tiniest openings. Everything was either getting damp or covered with a thin coating of ice. Even our breath froze as it came into contact with the canvas and then, owing to the incessant vibration of the tent, showered down on us again in the form of fine snow.

At times the angry squalls were followed by moments of complete stillness. These short periods of quiet between the longer stretches of fiendish din were exquisite. It was then that the monotonous voice of Guillermo became audible, reading out the New Testament to his companion. The bearers had otherwise not given

much evidence of themselves. Their morale appeared to have sagged badly in face of this visitation. They lay more or less apathetically in their little tent.

Terray took advantage of lulls to yell encouragement across. We heard unbelievingly that this could hardly be called a storm and that the wind was really nothing more than a strong breeze. Meanwhile he continued to busy himself as chef, melting snow and cooking macaroni. The day was endless and we all dreaded a second night of bedlam and sleeplessness. To combat this we had recourse to veronal, which at least helped us to doze off now and again. But our sleep was disturbed, and every extra-heavy gust brought us back to instant wakefulness.

When at length another new day broke we felt utterly exhausted. There was still no improvement in the weather: if anything, it was blowing harder than ever. Even Terray now had to admit this really *was* a blizzard. The infernal racket was getting me down, and I came to the conclusion that we simply had to seek some form of diversion, but not just to kill time, rather to make use of it. I therefore suggested to De Booy that this might be a favourable, if not exactly a quiet, opportunity for us to draw up—while we had this time on our hands—an outline of the book in which we intended to record our adventures in the Cordillera Blanca. De Booy did not think much of the idea and tried to persuade me that we could not possibly plan a book when we did not know whether we should ever succeed in scaling the Huantsán. But I refused to entertain the possibility of defeat. I argued with him lengthily and illogically. It was, I pleaded speciously, precisely at the moment when everything seemed so hopeless, that we had all the more reason to do something to bolster up our confidence. We could at least make draft plans on the offchance that success might be ours.

At last De Booy gave in. A pencil stub was unearthed from some bag and an empty gingerbread carton served as notepaper.

We spent hours that day drawing up a detailed scheme for a book

incorporating the successful climbing of the Huantsán as the main achievement of the expedition. The work really did take our minds off the blizzard. When, about midday, the pieces of cardboard were carefully tucked away in one of the rucksacks, we both felt satisfied that the morning had not been wasted. Our scrawl would probably be illegible as the result of writing lying down, with thick mittens on. But a book outline *had* been prepared. All that remained was to climb the Huantsán, and then we could fill in the gaps.

Terray, alone in his tent, found distraction much more difficult and was terribly bored. At first he amused himself by singing every song in his extensive repertoire at least three times. Fortunately most of his vocal effort was lost in the hullabaloo of the blizzard, but now and then snatches reached our ears. One ditty that he kept repeating ran: 'Il est dans la Hollande, les Hollandais l'ont pris.' He only remembered this one line, but it seemed appropriate for the occasion and to have a peculiar fascination for him. In fact, it so took his fancy that he must have repeated it well over a thousand times that day.

In the end, singing got on his nerves, too; so he crawled through the snow to share our company. De Booy had the bright idea of setting up the three-man tent which we held in reserve. All three of us could then be together and we could share the burden of cooking. Terray went over to the porters to see if they could lend a hand, but it appeared that nothing could be expected from them. They were utterly demoralized, complained of sundry pains, and wanted only to get away from this freezing pandemonium. We knew all along that Pelegrino was a weakling, so his attitude caused us no surprise. Guillermo told us later that all through the blizzard Pelegrino had refused to eat anything, but had continually doped himself with *Coca*, the dried leaf of a Peruvian plant, chewed locally as a narcotic stimulant. Even the stalwart Guillermo was too downhearted and dejected to want to tackle any camp work.

One could appreciate how terribly scared these half-Indians—

who had never before set foot on snow or ice—must have been by the roaring elements at this great height. We could not very well reproach them. They naturally viewed everything in another light, and one could not expect them to share our obsession about reaching the summit.

In the meantime De Booy and I put on every scrap of clothing we could find. As briskly as possible, we proceeded to put up the three-man Nanda Devi tent. It was freezing, as the Dutch say, 'till it cracked', and the wind was enough to cut one in two. The other tents were now almost completely lost in the snow. We gave the securing ropes a quick extra turn for safety, then tumbled hastily into the tent, our hands and feet absolutely dead with cold. It took a long time to thaw ourselves out. Our outer garments and also the bottom ends of the sleeping-bags were covered with a layer of ice. Worse still, the sleeping-bags had become damp inside.

Now that the three of us were together in one tent, our 'internment' was somewhat more bearable. Our own morale had gradually deteriorated too, although for very different reasons from the bearers'. It was now obvious that our second attempt on the Huantsán had failed, before we had begun the actual climb. Even if the next day were fine—which did not seem at all likely at the moment —we should nevertheless be forced to return to base camp, as a great quantity of provisions and cooking spirit had been consumed in the last few days. Moreover, it was impossible to spend confined days and nights at this high altitude without experiencing ill effects from lack of oxygen. We felt far more worn out than two days earlier, when we had come up, and regarded ourselves as in no fit state to start anything big. A thorough rest was indicated. We consoled each other with the thought that there was still time for a third attempt on the summit.

I had taken over the cooking that evening. For two hours I busied myself preparing a meal of meat and mashed potatoes, followed by stewed fruit. Outside the storm raged with unabated fury,

but queerly enough, we had become so used to the fearful noise that we now scarcely noticed it. After the meal, reconciled to the fact that our second attempt had failed, I snuggled down in my sleeping-bag and listened to Lionel's yarns. The trip had given me a new experience, one which I would not quickly forget. It also had the effect of knitting still more closely the bonds between our little team.

Terray showed himself appreciative of our company and expressed this by coming out with all sorts of intimate anecdotes. He was a first class raconteur with a typical French sense of humour. His straight from the shoulder style cheered us up no end. The candle had long been snuffed out, but one incredible yarn followed the other, until at last the double ration of sleeping pills began to take effect in Terray's case too. That night we all slept like logs. Tension was over, we had resigned ourselves to the inevitable.

We awoke next morning, July 1st, to find that the blizzard had ended, although the wind still swept at gale force. The sun soon broke through mists which were being wind-whipped into shreds. We were just beginning to melt some snow for the Milo malt drinks when, to our surprise, Pelegrino's head appeared in the tent-opening. He announced that he was definitely through with all this, and that Guillermo and he had decided to go down forthwith to base camp and to return from there to Ticapampa. He came to ask us to pay him his wages, as he assumed this was the last he would see of us.

For a moment all three of us were speechless. What could have been more incongruous than this request to settle up at six o'clock in the morning, 18,000 feet up, with a gale still blowing? And yet the demand had its serious side. If this fellow was really set on having his way and did attempt to go down, despite our warnings, it would be nothing less than suicidal. By now the wind and snow would, of course, have completely obliterated our previous track over the glacier, unsafe at the best of times. In such circumstances

After the fall. The bivouac on the west flank of the north ridge

De Booy, still far from fit, back at base camp.

Camp 2 at 18,040 feet

In the grip of the blizzard

the inexperienced fellows would not have a dog's chance of making a safe descent. There remained nothing for it, therefore, but to take advantage of the present favourable turn in the weather and go down with them.

Because of the danger of frost-bite it was necessary for us to postpone our departure until the sun rose higher and gave out more warmth. In that biting wind it was impossible to keep hands and feet warm. Terray went out for a few minutes to film the mist shreds which were being whisked with unbelievable rapidity up the face of the Huantsán. Almost immediately two of his fingers became numb. We had to massage them for him for quite a while before feeling returned.

By ten o'clock the weather had become somewhat better, so we decided to leave the tents in Camp 2, in the hope that they would stand up to any further battering by the wind which might take place. Only one of the two-man tents had collapsed—its poles had snapped during the night. This tent was therefore emptied. Even Pelegrino, who suddenly became active now that he knew we were going down, gave a hand. Actually it would have been better had he still remained aloof. He was taking one of the foam-plastic mattresses out of the tent, but could not have been holding it firmly enough, for the wind suddenly wrenched it from his grasp. A few moments later we saw the mattress sailing away high above us, caught up in a whirlwind. A minute later we could only just see it, hundreds of feet aloft, being dashed against the face of the Huantsán.

These mattresses were somewhat special. They were foam-plastic sheets, nearly 6 feet long and 2 feet wide. Although only one-fifth of an inch in thickness they gave complete protection from the rising cold. They were only $9\frac{1}{2}$ oz. in weight, so we were glad to take them with us to the higher camps and leave the heavier air-mattresses, which weighed nearly $2\frac{1}{4}$ lb., in the base camp. These plastic sheets could be regarded as a big advance towards the ideal

camp equipment, and Terray was most enthusiastic about them. It was therefore a shame to see one being whisked off to destruction.

Terray was furious. He spoke his mind to Pelegrino and no bones about it. If there was one thing that infuriated Terray it was lack of courage, and we now knew that this particular porter failed badly in this respect. Once we were back in the base camp and could review all the recent happenings in better perspective, we were more sympathetic and understanding of what it must have meant for the native porters to undergo such a fearful trial.

In the meantime De Booy had prepared a mug of hot Milo malt for each of us. It was important to get as warm as possible before attempting to brave the storm. One last look round, then off we went, making our way at good pace down the glacier. Everything went well. During the past night I had suffered a lot with cold feet and Terray and De Booy had taken turns to massage them for me. Now, by degrees, the continuous movement brought back a better circulation.

It was not until we had passed through the col that for the first time in three days we found ourselves more or less protected from the ferocious wind. We stood for a while, surprised to observe the sprightly way in which our porters, despite their sundry aches and pains, were getting along. The only thing they really suffered from was lack of morale. We had given them due warning in the beginning of the hardships which an undertaking such as ours inevitably entailed, but it was clear that this encounter with the Huantsán had proved altogether too much for them.

After a short rest in Camp 1 we put our best foot forward and towards noon approached the ice-fall, where it was necessary to put on crampons. Terray had given his to Pelegrino to carry and now asked for them back. At first Pelegrino acted as though he did not understand. Then he reluctantly confessed that he had left them behind in Camp 2. It was the last straw. We had never seen Terray in

such a towering rage. For the second time that day he poured forth on Pelegrino his full repertoire of abuse. Then he stormed ahead— without crampons—down the ice gully. Later Guillermo told us that Pelegrino actually had Terray's crampons with him all the time. He had left his own up there in Camp 2, but preferred to brave Terray's wrath rather than venture down the steep gully without crampons.

Back at length in base camp, we were received with enthusiasm by Blasido and Leucadio. It was fairly warm below, and our past privations were soon forgotten. But one glance up at the Huantsán left us in no doubt that the gale was still raging away up there. We had not expected to hear that Blasido and Leucadio had also been disturbed by the storm and were astonished when they said that for the first few days they, too, had not been able to venture outside the tents.

During our absence Blasido had gone down to San Marcos to buy potatoes and other provisions, leaving Leucadio on his own in the camp, an easy prey to loneliness and daunted by hardship. On returning, Blasido had to use all his powers of persuasion to prevail on him not to throw up the sponge altogether. It seemed too bad that one could place so little reliance on the Indian porters here in the Andes. We still had some differences to settle with Guillermo and Pelegrino, so I asked De Booy to take these two gentlemen properly in hand.

Guillermo was ashamed of his behaviour and only wanted a chance to rehabilitate himself. He declared himself ready to accompany us again to Camp 2, provided we would allow him to return below forthwith. If the weather remained good there was, of course, nothing against this. In any case, we were practically forced to agree, because the porter problem was now threatening to jeopardize our whole undertaking.

With Pelegrino matters were somewhat different. He was fed up to the teeth and totally unconcerned about the fact that he was

under contract to us. He pretended to be suffering agonies from toothache and simply had to return to Ticapampa to get treatment. Irritated though we all were by the wretched business, I nevertheless could not help laughing when I saw De Booy, a pair of pliers in his hand, making him open his mouth and examining his teeth one by one by torch-light. But Pelegrino stood his ground; so there was nothing for it but to let him go. He was under obligation to return the clothing issued to him in Ticapampa; but, of course, we could not turn him away stark-naked; so we made out a list of everything he had received from us and made him sign it. Next morning, when we awoke, we discovered that he had already disappeared, taking with him a whole box of bars of chocolate.

This was not the first occasion that Pelegrino had bolted. Once, without bothering about his pay, he had gone off, only to be hauled back half an hour later by Guillermo and threatened with prosecution if he violated his contract. His disappearance was, however, as we later appreciated, all to the good, for his everlasting grousing had a bad influence on the other porters, particularly on the poor-spirited Leucadio. We were pretty sure that Guillermo's poor morale during the blizzard was mainly due to sharing a tent with Pelegrino for over sixty hours.

For all that, we were very much concerned about our porter strength being so reduced. Leucadio was a poor specimen as a bearer, but was useful as a hunter. We used to send him out every day to replenish our pot with fresh meat, as his prowess with the gun enabled us to reserve our small stock of tinned foods for the third Huantsán attempt. As a hunter Leucadio proved first class, though it was a mystery to us how he managed with his ancient muzzle-loader. During our stay at the base camp we lived so well on Vizcacha (a sort of rabbit) and wild duck that we almost got tired of them.

Individually we now tried to build up our stamina in anticipation of the great test ahead. We busied ourselves—each to his liking—

with all sorts of occupations. De Booy concentrated on the stores and made comprehensive lists of the remaining provisions. Terray spent his time reading. Anticipating the need for light literature when resting in base camp, De Booy and I had included a small stock of books in our expeditionary inventory; but we forgot to bring any French books for Terray. This unfortunate omission meant that our *ami* had to fall back on English books. He had borrowed a book from me, *No Orchids for Miss Blandish*, but his restricted knowledge of English resulted in his invoking my aid every few minutes. This was rather a liability. I was busy writing articles and already had difficulty enough concentrating on the job, for my mind kept straying to the Huantsán, that great mountain which looked so near and yet was so far. Whilst my gaze rested on its lofty summit, my thoughts went back to the fall, the bivouac, the blizzard. In spite of all our efforts, we had as yet attained nothing.

De Booy and I worked out that his fall during the night of June 21st had in all probability saved our lives. If everything had gone according to plan on that occasion we should have returned to Camp 1 the next day. Allowing for several days' rest there, including the establishment of Camp 2, we should probably have commenced the all-out assault on the ridge on June 25th, establishing Camp 3 that same evening somewhere up at the 20,000-ft. level. June 26th and 27th would have found us negotiating the saddle between the north and south summits and attempting the higher summit.

Thus we should inevitably have been caught high up on the mountain when the blizzard descended in all its fury during the night of June 28th–29th. It was easy to imagine what could have happened. Even if the hurricane had not swept us, tents and all, from the ridge, we should in all probability have been trapped by the blizzard. And had we still managed by the skin of our teeth to survive, there was little doubt that the descent of the north-west ridge with all its terrible complications would have proved altogether too much for us in our weakened state, quite apart from the

constant danger of frost-bite. What is more, our stock of provisions and spirit for the stove would also have run out long before then. In the light of events it was no overstatement to say that De Booy's fall proved actually a blessing in disguise. In fact, we were all grateful for the bizarre way in which fate had dealt with us.

THE NORTH SUMMIT

It was some time before the weather returned to normal. The sky remained overcast and for several days after our return to base camp the wind seemed to blow from all quarters, except of course the right one. Little by little we completely recovered; in fact, things began to bore us down there below. Then, on the morning of July 3rd, the clouds scurried across the sky in a favourable direction, and there was no holding us back. Out we set again for a third attack on the mountain. But we were too presumptuous. By the time we reached the ice-fall the sky had darkened and it began to rain gently. A brief council was held. Should we go on or turn back? Terray pointed to the clouds being driven in a westerly direction from the Amazon plain—always a bad omen. To continue now would not be reasonable. It would be foolish to risk being confined in one of the camps at high altitude, frittering away our present high standard of physical fitness, so glumly we returned to base camp.

As it happened the weather improved a lot during the course of that day. The evening was so fine and clear that we regretted having been so cautious. 'C'est le grand beau temps,' said Lionel. 'I don't care what happens, we are definitely going to start that attack to-morrow!'

Next day it looked as if a change for the better had definitely set in. The cloud ceiling was still fairly heavy, but the wind had veered round to just the right direction. More important still, the moun-

tains themselves looked as though they were far away—a very good indication of settled conditions.

We left base camp at eight accompanied by the three heavily-laden porters, and soon we were passing, for the umpteenth time, the dangerous ice-fall with its rickety séracs. Lionel pressed on ahead with the bearers, for it was intended that they should go up and return to base camp that same day.

Up to that time I had been in exceptionally good condition, but now I felt somewhat out of sorts. Toiling laboriously upwards, I perspired freely—a thing which had never troubled me before in the dry atmosphere of the Cordillera Blanca. Every step of the route to Camp 1 was by now imprinted on my memory, but it all somehow went against the grain. There was something depressing about it. The glacier, the snow, the rarefied air—they all seemed hostile.

De Booy, noticing my depression, tried to buck me up. No one had rejoiced more in my previous excellent condition than he. With a few choice encouraging words he managed to raise my spirits. He, himself, was in the best of form. He told me that he had felt in his bones—long before the blizzard overtook us—that our second attempt, like the first, would fail. And his foreboding had come true. Now, however, he was confident that everything was going to be fine and that we were going to reach that summit. As a rule, I set very little faith in such premonitions, one way or the other; but De Booy's cheery optimism was infectious.

Presently we passed the place where Camp 1 had been located and picked up what provisions still remained there. That day we took everything fairly easy. Terray and the porters were far in front and already nearing Camp 2 about the time De Booy and I reached the col leading to the westerly glacier. When we met the porters on their return journey to base camp we still had an hour's climb ahead. They were as pleased as Punch and obviously looking forward to an easy time down below. A few warning words from me

urging them to take great care and, above all, to keep up a good pace in order to pass that ice-fall in daylight, and they pressed on with their descent. At the approach to the col, they waved back once more before finally going out of sight. From now on we were alone on the mountain. From now on we had to do everything ourselves. Our last contact with the outside world was cut.

Arriving in Camp 2, we found Terray busy as a bee, trying to bring a little order into the chaos. The tents left behind in the blizzard had been partly blown over and covered with thick snowdrifts. All sorts of things haphazardly left lying about owing to the porters' stampede after the blizzard, had now to be unearthed, search being specially made for a Corsican leather flask, filled with alcohol, which we needed badly for cooking purposes. According to Guillermo, it had been left outside the tent by Pelegrino. Our supply of alcohol was meagre, so for over an hour De Booy and Terray slogged away clearing snow from the entire camp. But all their efforts were in vain. Pelegrino had undoubtedly pinched the flask, and not only just for its contents. The snow-shifting was not altogether unfruitful, however, for my crampons, as well as those issued to Pelegrino, came to light.

But we were forced to reserve our limited supplies of alcohol for use in the higher camps. So now we had recourse to our petrol stove—a proceeding which once again nearly caused a catastrophe. This type of stove always does the unexpected. Suddenly, out from it shot a long streak of flame, and it was only thanks to the split-second reaction of De Booy that a serious tent-fire was avoided. With one lightning movement of his arm he sent the whole contraption flying into the open.

Lionel, who always strongly disapproved of our casual way of handling petrol, particularly after what happened on the Pongos, now raised Cain again, ranting on about the horrors of losing tents at high altitudes. The atmosphere was excellent, to be sure. Long after the candle had been blown out we had to listen to his tales of

Camp 3 at 19,350 feet. In the background the south pyramid of the Huantsán—taken at dawn

woe and tribulation. That night it was not so much high altitude as nervous tension which kept us long awake.

The new day brought perfect weather. After a breakfast of porridge and gingerbread, we got down to the job of sharing out the loads. Here we missed the powerful Guillermo, whose rucksack, packed always to capacity, did much to lighten our own. Now we had to carry everything ourselves, and not merely over a simple glacier, but up steep ice.

Three hours were spent in sorting everything out, and even when we had reduced our baggage to the absolute minimum, there still remained a considerable weight for each of us to shoulder. One could not economize on such things as clothes and pitons. As for provisions we had to allow for the possibility of bad weather, so we took enough food for seven days, a quantity which actually proved anything but too much. The three-man Nanda Devi tent had to be taken, together with sleeping-bags, plastic mattresses, and a deal of photographic and filming material. Then there were such indispensable items as kletterhammers, two 200-ft. nylon ropes, and bivouac sets. In the end, each of us had to lug along rucksacks weighing about 55 lb.

In the old days—before the advent of nylon and plastic materials and other boons to the present-day mountaineer in the shape of light, durable equipment—the same items and gear would have been at least double the weight. It is no exaggeration to say that twenty years ago the very thought of a party of only three climbers attempting such a long arduous climb as the Huantsán, carrying everything themselves, would have been regarded as sheer idiocy.

In view of my privileged position in the middle of the rope the big tent fell to my lot, and, oh, how often in the days that followed did I bless that big, awkward thing. It was always doing its darnedest to pull me off my balance.

By ten o'clock we were through and able to set off. One final glance at the two small tents remaining in Camp 2—and the great

On the way to the north summit—the only flat part of the Huantsán

climb began! Problems cropped up almost immediately. This north-west ridge might well have a somewhat less dangerous cornice than the north ridge, but its flanks were horribly steep. Below us the abyss, particularly on the north flank, was terrifying.

To reach the crest we had to overcome our first obstacle, an ice-wall sloping up at an angle of about 55 degrees. Lionel, as leader, took it in great style, without cutting a single step with his axe. As always, it was a sight for sore eyes to watch him negotiate the wall on his crampons. Elegant as a ballet dancer, without a single unnecessary movement, he gave one the impression that there was really nothing to it. But how illusory that impression was, I soon found out in the next few minutes when it came to my turn. And that was but a foretaste of the complications which were to beset us all day long—difficult ice-work, where everything depended on balance (and we were burdened with those excessively heavy rucksacks). Half-way up the wall, I had to cut a couple of steps and then, cheered on by De Booy, I struggled on up to the crest.

Then, whilst Terray went on ahead, I sat astride the *arête* and gave the signal for De Booy to come up. I rammed my axe into the snow to the handle and with a turn of the rope used it as a belay. This was a critical moment for De Booy. It was his first big technical effort since the fall, and I wondered anxiously whether he still retained all his old self-confidence. From my perch I could not see him, so could only judge his progress by the rate at which I took in the rope. It seemed an age. Now and then I could hear him cutting steps and assumed that he was finding the going difficult. I accordingly yelled out to him encouragingly. Then things went quicker, and after some minutes his head came in view. I had been worrying for nothing. The delay half-way up had been caused by his nearly losing the filming apparatus from the big breast pocket in front of his anorak. It was there so as to be easily to hand for taking action shots higher up the *arête*. At the trickiest part of the wall the camera somehow or other got loose. Luckily it was attached to a thin cord

which went round De Booy's neck and that saved it from smashing down on the glacier.

There was no chance to hold an inquest, for Terray kept shouting to me to follow on. We could now see the *arête* ahead, but it looked anything but pleasant. I recalled Terray's remark that he did not think there would be any insurmountable problems at this point. A few rope lengths along, a break occurred in the cornice and it was possible to follow the crest itself. But this luxury did not last long, and we were soon forced on to the sharply pitched west flank. Here the snow appeared to be in ideal condition and the points of our crampons found firm footholds, which was a great relief, for the slope fell away at an angle of over 60 degrees, dropping sheerly down towards the clearly delineated Rajucolta and Shallap valleys, more than 5,000 feet below.

We now had to contend with shortness of breath. But the greatest handicap was the heavy rucksack, the leather straps of which bit deep into the shoulders, particularly when climbing steep sections, for then one was obliged to raise both arms at every other step in order to drive the axe with full force into the snow. The snow was so hard that sometimes one had to strike several times before the axe went deep enough to provide adequate support. But on and on! Up and up!

I forced myself to stop thinking too much about things and tried to carry out all the requisite climbing manœuvres with the least possible output of energy. In the course of years of mountaineering I had acquired this knack of applying a sort of 'mental blackout' to myself in moments of extreme difficulty. This practice stood me now in good stead. I consoled myself, too, with the thought that as the days went by and the rations were consumed, so would the weight of the rucksacks diminish.

All sense of time was lost in that exhausting climb. On and on! At four in the afternoon we reached a small ledge. Even here it was a job to find sufficient room to sit down. Before we could find a

place on which to put the rucksacks with safety we had to hack away a good deal of snow with the axe. The heavy weight of the rucksacks made them almost unmanageable, and we fully appreciated how easily they could slide away and vanish into the depths. The loss of any one of the rucksacks would, of course, put a finish to the attempt, so we belayed them as securely as possible to well-rammed-in axes.

Later on, De Booy told us how the buckle of a shoulder-strap had worked loose during the climb. Luckily, it had happened during a simple passage, otherwise the incident might have deprived him of the rucksack and all three of us of victory over the Huantsán. Not only each rucksack, but also each axe was a vital necessity, to be held on to like grim death. During the rest periods we always rammed them in with the greatest care.

We looked up at the stretch still to be negotiated that day. Up to now the *arête* had been extremely narrow, but higher up it gradually broadened. This was an advantage, as we could proceed the rest of the way without being hindered by cornice dangers. As against that, the crest became steeper and steeper until, at the shoulder of the mountain, it culminated in a very steep and smooth wall. From our resting place we now had a splendid view of the north ridge. It was plain that, however complicated our route that day had been, its difficulties were nothing compared to the north ridge, which was heavily jagged in its lower portions, while higher up it was entirely fringed with overhanging cornices. We were now all the more convinced that the north-west ridge was the key to the climbing of the Huantsán. In fact, it looked the only possible route up which a small group of climbers could bring, fairly rapidly, sufficient equipment and stores to a suitable site for an assault camp.

We had counted on reaching such a site that day. Only two hours of daylight were left, but we felt that the nastiest problems of the day were now behind us. From a climbing point of view our rate of progress that day had been agonizingly slow. In six gruelling

hours we had only gained about 1,000 feet in height. We had not given ourselves a single pause for rest and one or the other of us had been on the move all the time, so the technical difficulties can well be imagined.

Even now Lionel did not grant us much time to recover our breath. He had misgivings about possible complications higher up, and urged us to make speed. Very likely he was also concerned lest the reactions of this exhausting day should set in too strongly before we reached our camp site.

The first few slopes went fairly well, though they were so steep that our leader was repeatedly forced to cut steps. Then everything became more and more wearisome. The day's severe physical strain now began to take its toll. I had all the work in the world to make myself concentrate on the technical tasks in hand. As usual, we had underestimated the actual distance to be covered, and for a time we were scared that we should be caught *en route* by nightfall. Then, just as dusk began to close in on the mountain, things panned out all right. Lionel reached the shoulder and called out to me that we had 'arrived'. One last strenuous effort and I was there, too. De Booy could now follow.

It was bitterly cold up there. The day's slogging efforts had kept us so warm that we still had thin garments on; but the moment one stayed still the chill wind cut through and through. For some reason or other, it seemed to me that De Booy was taking a heck of a time to catch up. Benumbed with cold, I called out to him to put a move on for Pete's sake, and what the deuce was he playing at, it wasn't a bit difficult, I had done that last section in far less time! I must have lost all sense of proportion. When he eventually reached us, he roundly accused me in turn of having taken much more time negotiating that last bit. It was a toss-up which of us was right. We finally just had to laugh it off. The important thing was that we had managed to reach our day's objective. Success in this materially increased our confidence in ultimate victory. More im-

portant still, the day had shown that all three of us were in excellent shape.

The first sight that met our eyes on this slightly-tilted plateau was a fairly distant pyramid thrusting itself fantastically into the night sky. I rubbed my eyes in amazement. What on earth was this? What mountain was there of that particular architecture and dimension in the vicinity? Then it slowly dawned upon me: this was the south summit of the Huantsán. It had previously been obscured by the shoulder of the mountain. I was still in a state of doubtful hesitation when Lionel definitely confirmed the situation.

Then other thoughts took shape. This peak looked so far away that to reach and climb it would be impossible in one day. . . . Or was the distance magnified in the semi-dark? So this was the south summit and there to the left was the ridge up which we would have to climb! It looked far worse than the *arête* up which we had so laboriously toiled that day. Or was I now so desperately tired, bodily and mentally, that I could not see things in their true perspective?

In the vague light the steep pinnacle, partially shrouded in mists, appeared the very embodiment of inaccessibility. It looked almost unreal, not part of this world at all, a castle in the air, a bridge to heaven. I felt, subconsciously perhaps, that this was a picture I should keep for ever; and although my companions stood there silent and awe-struck, too, absorbed in this wondrous spectacle, I had the feeling that somehow it belonged solely to me—to me alone.

But there was little time to let one's thoughts go dallying in such fantasies. Plodding on to the place where we intended pitching Camp 3, we sank to our knees in snow. The tent had to be set up without delay, and that was quite a job in itself. The snow was so soft and powdery that the aluminium tent pegs could not be driven in securely. We were obliged to dig a trench, going deeper and deeper before we came to a hard layer of snow. Even then we had

to use axes and ice-pitons instead of the normal tent-pegs. While we were busy, night descended and the cold became so unbearable that we hastily sought the shelter of the tent and crept into our sleeping-bags. The meal that night was confined to a bare minimum. After the nerve-racking day none of us was very hungry, and long before eight o'clock we had fallen asleep.

Towards midnight I was awakened by the flapping of the tent canvas. A strong wind had arisen, and I could not easily get off to sleep again. The frequent gusts brought back vivid memories of the blizzard which had marooned us in Camp 2, and at each fresh impact I tried to judge whether it was more powerful than its predecessor. I lay awake—perhaps ten minutes, maybe several hours—it seemed a long time. In the end, fatigue blurred my anxious gauging of the force of the wind. I must have dozed off, for the next thing I knew was that Terray's alarm watch was shrilling and it was five o'clock in the morning. At first, I hardly realized where I was. Then my attention focused itself on the weather. Cheers! Stars were visible through the tent opening and the sky was cloudless. The cold was unbelievable, its keen bite accentuated by a strong wind. Metal things, such as axes, crampons, spoons, etc., tended to stick to one's hands. The temperature was minus 15° C.

Dawn was a revelation. As the sun's first rays caressed the crown of the south summit, long shadows were cast on the mountain face. We stood outside the tent, enraptured by the exquisite beauty of it all. It was a good opportunity to study our surroundings. The south pyramid now seemed much nearer than on the previous night, and the ridge also looked far less savage by daylight. At its lower sections it was practically free from cornice, but higher up, this grim menace of the Andes appeared again in full force. There, above the steep north-west face, were poised the threatening gigantic ice-curtains. It was clear that when the decisive attack was on to-morrow, cornices of such magnitude would inevitably force us on to the very uninviting east face.

Veering round to the north summit, which was hardly 650 feet above our camp, we saw that the ridge looked simple, so the day in front of us should be fairly easy. The night before, we had taken our mountaineering boots to bed with us, pushing them down to the bottom of our sleeping-bags in order to thaw them out. Pulling them out now, it seemed as if even this precautionary measure had been inadequate, for they were still partly frozen and we had a lot of trouble pulling the stiff leather over our feet.

After a frugal breakfast of rice and Milo malt beverages—we had unfortunately forgotten to bring up oatmeal for porridge-making—we put on all our available clothing and broke camp. Towards eight o'clock we began the journey which would take us over the north summit and down to the saddle at the foot of the south summit. Up the slope we climbed through the soft snow. Before we came to the ridge leading directly to the north summit, we had to go over the shoulder, and at first this was quite a pleasant passage. But the higher we went the mushier became the snow. Terray, in the lead as usual, sank to his knees at every step. The route was, of course, simple technically, but this everlasting sinking in the snow made it extremely tiresome.

Arriving at the *arête*, we followed this into the north-east flank, where the snow was somewhat crisper. At many places the hard upper crust held Terray's weight. But I, weighing three or four stone more, always went through the upper crust and often sank to my knees in the snow, although I carefully trod in each of Terray's footsteps. Apparently Terray did not realize that I, like him in effect, was now stamping out a track, for when I called out to him after a time pleading for a slightly slower pace, to my great annoyance he accused me of lagging. The lighter De Booy, last on the rope, had it much easier. He could step into my track without the slightest fear of sinking in further. This was about the only time, he told me later, that he'd had things break his way so comfortably.

De Booy could not quite understand why we were not making

View of the San Juan (centre) and other unclimbed ice-giants

better progress. At one stage he said to me: 'This must be one of Terray's "off days"! He usually puts up a much better show than this!'

A little later I had to laugh inwardly when Lionel, wishing to reserve his energies somewhat for the expected trials ahead, asked De Booy to take the lead for a while. De Booy began with such a rush that I had the utmost difficulty trying to keep up with him. With all due respect to his stamina, I nevertheless had the feeling that this pace wouldn't last long. So I said nothing. And, just as I anticipated, after a little while the pace slowed down considerably. Another fifteen minutes and he had to stop and sit down, utterly fagged out.

Glad as I was of that respite, I couldn't help teasing Terray with what De Booy had recently said about his tempo. At first Terray was inclined to be indignant; then he realized that De Booy's speedy exhaustion was really a big feather in his cap. Mollified, he took the lead again, conscious that neither of us in future would ever dare challenge his pace. To query his performance touched his honour too nearly. Terray was terribly prestige-conscious and a lot had to happen before he would admit that anyone could even possess equal stamina.

As far as I was concerned, the pace that day could not be too slow. Quite apart from that tiresome sagging in the soft snow, the trip was proving exceedingly trying for me. I suffered continually from lack of oxygen. The previous punishing day and my bad night in Camp 3 also, undoubtedly, contributed their repercussive ill effects. It was no ordinary tiredness, for when I stood still I felt quite all right. It was more a disinclination to exert myself, as if my limbs were shackled with lead weights, which I just could not shake off.

In any case, the climb seemed unending and I was near the end of my tether when the north summit was at last reached. Actually it was little more than the culmination of the long, gently-tilted

Camp 4 at 19,850 feet, with the north summit (20,056 feet) of the Huantsán in the background

north ridge. At one o'clock Terray was the first to wave his axe above the lofty crown, which registered 20,056 feet. De Booy and I congratulated ourselves on having climbed our first 20,000-footer.

Just before joining Terray at the summit, I played the leading role in a short tragi-comedy. De Booy had called out that he was going to film my arrival on the north summit and that he would take a shot of me there, shaking hands with Terray. Summoning all my strength I rushed up the last bit, head well up, hand outstretched. But lurking treacherously in the last 30-ft. lap to the summit was a snow-covered crevasse, into which I nearly disappeared. I just managed to save myself waist-deep by driving my axe into the snow as far as it would go. But photographically it was all up with me. Whilst I awkwardly struggled to restore my equilibrium, De Booy, with real sadism, immortalized my plight in coloured film. Later, much to my relief and to my companions' chagrin, this particular section of film turned out a failure.

SUCCESS—THE SOUTH SUMMIT

After a short rest, the time came for the descent from the north summit to the saddle. According to Terray, this should provide the key to the climbing of the Huantsán. We had already seen from below that this was going to be a particularly steep part. It was true that, by one means or another, we could have descended by a series of rappels. But the real problem was not so much the present descent as the later ascent. If the latter was impracticable, it meant the end of the present assault. In fact, in that case, any chance of reaching the main summit of the Huantsán that year would be ruined.

As soon as we left the north summit our troubles began. First we had to work our way for some 40 feet or so down a particularly narrow *arête*, which suddenly fell sharply away on all sides. It all looked fearfully precarious. De Booy and I were greatly relieved to

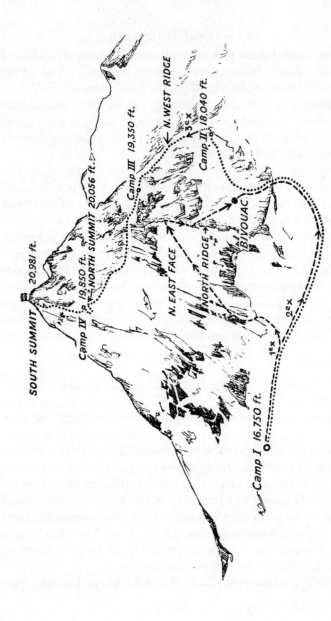

Sketch of the route to the Huantsán summit, showing assault camps I–4,
the north and north-west ridges, the north-east face, and site of bivouac.

see Lionel getting ready straight away to make an attempt to find a spot lower down, from where a traverse in the direction of the saddle might be possible. The slope was thickly covered with snow and perilously steep. I looked inquiringly at De Booy. As last man on the rope, he would have the far from enviable prospect of coming down unsecured, and he was not precisely looking forward to it. I gave him an encouraging nod.

Terray crawled slowly and warily down into the depths, his face turned to the wall. Repeatedly he drove his axe as far as it would go into the snow. The slope fell away here at an angle of 60 degrees down some 3,000 sheer feet to the glacier on which Camp 1 had been situated. Then he disappeared from view behind a projecting ice shelf. A little later came his muffled instructions to me to follow. Securely belayed by De Booy, I went down about 50 feet and was just beginning to overcome that fluttering 'fly on the wall' feeling, when Terray suddenly reappeared below me. He signalled me to return to the ridge. His 'impossible' sounded somewhat oppressive. Another fifteen minutes saw all three of us back on the ridge.

Did this mean the end of the climb? Would we have to abandon everything now that we were so near to our goal? Was it too complicated? Not for Terray! After each of our previous failures he had maintained: 'Mais tout de même nous vaincrons, parce que nous sommes les plus forts!' Once again his confidence was contagious.

A moment later, belayed with extra special care, he was off on a new *recce*. The west face appeared still less promising than the east, if only by reason of the enormous cornice poised over the former. Terray decided therefore to try and force his way down the ice-wall where the *arête* broke off so abruptly. Shortly afterwards he disappeared behind a narrow ice-crest. De Booy and I remained above in almost unbearable suspense, hearing only the irregular blows of his axe and his curt orders to pay out the rope.

To us, the anxious waiting seemed endless. At last the whole rope

length of 200 feet was paid out, and I was getting ready to follow on down, when there came a sudden request to haul in the rope. A few minutes later Terray's red beret came in view. We were surprised to get the good news that there was a distinct possibility of winning a way down the ice-wall. Terray asked De Booy whether he was willing to go down last, but De Booy was honest enough to admit that he would prefer being securely belayed on such a hazardous manœuvre. I fully appreciated his point of view, for the dizzy depths below were breath-taking.

Once again we altered the order. De Booy went down first, negotiating the 200 feet by means of the steps that Terray had expertly cut in the ice-wall. Snow lay here and there, but hard blue ice showed through everywhere. It was absolutely impossible to drive in an axe for security, so notwithstanding the steps the descent demanded the utmost concentration. But our most acute problem had been solved. Not only were we able to descend to the saddle, but our ascent on the return journey was now assured. The operation had taken about two hours. We had still 300 to 400 feet to contour before we could reach the saddle itself. A steep ice-ridge was easily negotiated. Sloping snowfields, criss-crossed with treacherous snowed-over crevasses, now lay in front. We went over one very weak snow-bridge by pushing ourselves forward on our tummies in order to spread the weight as much as possible. At last we came to the saddle.

Terray wanted to utilize the hours that still separated us from dusk by climbing the first slopes leading to the south summit. I agreed, but as *quid pro quo* secured the luxury of a short rest. Now that the nerve-racking strain was over, we could more fully enjoy the superb view. Behind us lay the north summit, sharply silhouetted against the clear sky. We looked with satisfaction at the steep ice-wall we had just descended.

In front of us tiered up a mighty bastion, the south summit, its sharp ascending ridge soaring high above us, cutting the sky. Ter-

ray, who had by now dismissed the north summit from his mind, was concentrating on the route to be taken next day. Several steeply-pitched snow slopes reached up to the ridge and as we had seen from Camp 3, the ridge was scalable for about 1,000 feet up, then came the massive cornices which would force us inexorably on the steep east face. It looked imposing, but not entirely impossible.

As usual, it was Terray who interrupted our meditations and re-called us to reality. At that moment I could have cussed him—only to admit, five minutes later, how right he was. It was best to get under way, however tired one felt, for sitting afforded one no real rest. We slowly climbed the first slope. The snow was deep, but hard enough to enable one to make a track through it without sink-ing too deeply. Coming to a plateau, I thought that now at last our toil for that day was over and was just about to relieve my poor shoulders of the cutting straps of that wretched rucksack, but no!—Terray was still not satisfied. He wanted to go further, to the last level snowfield at the foot of the ridge. To-day, he said, we have the time; but no one can foretell how things would turn out to-morrow.

It was all right once we were again plodding on. Yet I had the feeling, tired though I was, that I had become very much more acclimatized that day. Although the slope we were now ascending was pretty stiff, shortness of breath was certainly not proving the handicap it had been first thing that morning.

When we finally reached a suitable site it was half-past four. De Booy and I shared the task of setting up Camp 4 at an altitude of about 19,850 feet, while Terray, amazing fellow, still with heaps of energy, took advantage of the remaining hour and a half of day-light to go several hundred yards up the ridge and prepare a route for to-morrow.

He returned just before dusk to find the camp ready for the night and a meal cooked. Needless to say, all three of us by then felt pretty well spent. In this state we could easily, at that high altitude,

have given way to a sort of jumpy testiness; but, as always, the atmosphere remained excellent.

I, myself, was perturbed over my poor form during the day. Although it had improved as the hours went by, I wondered uneasily whether there would be any repetition of that off-colour feeling in the morning. I had succeeded in getting up to Camp 4 and, as far as I was aware, had not—up to now—acted as a serious brake on my companions. It would, of course, be heartbreaking not to go on, to be compelled to give up, after so much intense effort, now that victory was in sight. All the same, it would only be the right thing to do if my presence was likely to jeopardize the success of our undertaking. I put it to Terray and asked what he thought. His answer was: 'This isn't a mountain to be taken lightly, Kees! If you're not up to the mark in the morning, then you cannot possibly come—however wretched it will be for all of us. But if you're feeling O.K., then come along! Technically, you can do it!'

This was enough for me. There was no cause to worry about the mountain. All I had to do was build up strength during the coming night. I forced myself to eat a good meal, although appetite invariably vanished at great height. In fact, the meat and rice simply revolted us. The tins of fruit which we had determinedly carried up with us, in spite of their heavy weight, were all we could enjoyably stomach.

The night sky was crystal clear. It was dreadfully cold. Our breath condensed on the walls of the tent, froze immediately, and then fell on us in the form of fine snow whenever the canvas shook in the wind.

Our experience with boots the night before had taught us a lesson. They had remained frozen, even though we had tried to thaw them in the ends of our sleeping-bags. This time we commenced operations with a pocket-knife, hacking off the clumps of ice frozen to our boots. Then we put the boots between our knees in the sleeping-bags in order to thaw them with our own bodily

147

warmth. Uncomfortable though this was, it was preferable to running the risk next day of suffering frost-bite during the final assault. It was best, at any rate, not to commence with cold feet.

After taking two veronal tablets I went off soundly to sleep. In the middle of the night, however, I was roused by the bitter cold. My hands were so icy that I was obliged to put on gloves. My face smarted and I suspected that my nose was beginning to get frost-bitten, so I wrapped a spare down-jacket belonging to Terray round my head. He and De Booy were able to snug down—head and all—in their sleeping-bags, but I unfortunately was too tall for that. The veronal tablets were still effective apparently, for I started to doze off again. My last vague thoughts were about having my own special sleeping-bag made for the next expedition, a longer and wider one.

With those wretched boots between our knees we could not twist or turn. But any restlessness was, in any case, impossible because of our positions in the tent. Terray and I lay on the outside and De Booy in the middle. Both Terray and I had a habit of rolling as far away from the icy-cold tent walls as possible, so that poor De Booy got precious little room in the middle. On one occasion, just out of curiosity, we measured the actual space he occupied and found it was barely eight inches, hardly sufficient to allow him to lie on his side. De Booy tended naturally to moan about this, but Terray and I used to pull his leg, saying we would gladly change places as he was certainly in the warmest position. We called him a chronic egoist, and made out that such grousing was outrageous.

Next morning, July 7th, Terray's alarm watch went off at 6.30. It was exceptionally cold, so we decided to lie on until the sun came through. Half an hour later, De Booy got up to prepare breakfast. We had never made an 'official' division of duties, but it had become the accepted thing that I should do the cooking at night-times while De Booy took turn in the mornings. Terray, who undertook the heaviest work during the day, was freed of all camp

The ascent. *Top:* Terray
Middle: De Booy *Bottom:* Egeler

fatigues. I still don't know what is worse: to squirm on one's stomach in a sleeping-bag for several hours trying to cook under difficulties when one is dead-tired after a heavy day's climbing; or to face the bleak cold at crack of dawn and shiveringly prepare breakfast while your companions are still lying there, luxuriously warm in their sleeping-bags.

The night's rest had done me the world of good. I felt enormously refreshed and almost forgot that we were nearly up to the 20,000-ft. level. But we were sharply reminded of the altitude when it came to dressing. Getting boots on involved quite a struggle and made us exhaustingly short of breath. That morning we put on every scrap of clothing we had brought. The wind had freshened up the previous night and was still blowing now with undiminished force.

Towards eight o'clock everything was at last ready. One great blessing, there was no need this time to lug along burdensome rucksacks! Tent, sleeping-bags and provisions—all were being left behind in camp. The final decisive attack was on! Before us rose the proud Huantsán in all its lofty splendour. Would we scale that glittering peak? All three of us were in good heart.

At first, rapid progress was made up the route prepared by Terray the night before, but as the slope became steeper our tempo slowed. Compared with the previous day I was a new man. Maybe I was more sensitive than the others to relatively small changes in altitude. A good night's rest, however, always seemed to work wonders; and happily that had happened again at this considerable height.

After climbing up the right flank of the ridge for a hundred yards or so, we planned to cross over the crest, as the east flank of the *arête*, although very steep, seemed the most suitable. For safety's sake we would have to move only one at a time. Terray, who had sized up the situation the previous night, straddled the crest and soon disappeared from view. Alert for his signal, I was getting ready to follow when we saw him making his way as fast as cir-

149

The south summit (20,981 feet) of the Huantsán. Most of the ascent was made up the ridge in the middle

cumstances would allow back to us. De Booy and I could not at first make out what had happened. Then he called out: 'I've got a frost-bitten foot!'

On joining us, he immediately took his boot off and we saw that his toes had turned white. To make sure of things, the other boot also came off. While Terray himself saw to one foot, De Booy massaged the other. I myself could not help, for while standing about waiting, my own feet had also become affected. For thirty whole minutes I frantically twiddled my toes about—piano playing—to induce normal circulation to return.

It is amazing how unnoticed, and with what rapidity, one's extremities can freeze. One minute everything is normal, the next minute the toes suddenly go dead. Stationed as now, on the sheltered side of the ridge, it was difficult to realize how intensely cold it was. The protection from wind made it all the more treacherous. But the brief time spent by Terray on the other side of the ridge, exposed to the full force of the wind, had been quite sufficient. Neither De Booy nor I had reckoned with such rapidity. In Holland everyone knows what it is to get dead feet when skating, but after a time the discomfort disappears. Out in the Andes it is a different kettle of fish altogether. Here the discomfort does not disappear on its own. Thank goodness, we could benefit from Terray's ripe experience on this score! He did not take the threat of frost-bite at all lightly. His reactions were instantaneous and energetic. During the next few days I was to learn a lot about frost-bite by painful personal experience.

After forty-five minutes or so Terray was at last satisfied; and the climb was on again. The loss of time had one good result: the sun had meanwhile risen much higher. Terray strongly recommended our wiggling our toes to maintain blood circulation.

But this was easier said than done. The ideal mountaineering boots have yet to be discovered. The difficulty is, of course, that the ideal boots have to satisfy two diametrically opposed requirements.

Firstly, climbers would like boots that are roomy enough to allow of their wearing several pairs of feet-warming socks at a time and roomy enough, too, to permit a degree of movement of the toes— that wiggling so strongly recommended by Terray. Secondly, climbers want their boots to be close-fitting, so that they do not give at all or slop, particularly during difficult climbs when crampons are required. As this second demand is all-important it must at present be accorded top priority, and one has necessarily to forgo the warmth and comfort of roominess.

Crossing over the ridge, we came directly in the teeth of the icy wind. For another hundred yards we followed the route prepared by Terray, climbing straight upwards and steadily steeper. Then the prepared route ended and we had to tackle *terra incognita*. Snow conditions were excellent, so for a time we were able to make good progress. Then the snow layer became thinner and blue ice, protruding here and there, indicated the need for extreme care. At one point a passage of only thirty feet or so cost much precious time. Luckily, higher up, we were able to pick up speed, even though the *arête* remained appallingly steep. But we were coming closer and closer to the top.

Nevertheless, it was unthinkable that the Huantsán was going to surrender all that lightly. We thought uneasily of the cornice ahead, which was going to force us off the ridge on to the steep flank.

An overhanging shelf of ice made us traverse on to the west flank and we abruptly came face to face with a vertical ice-wall which looked anything but simple. Here again, Terray exhibited his verve and master-craft. In the space of a few minutes he climbed up no less than 60 feet of ice-wall while De Booy took a colour film of the feat. We always filmed everything of this nature that we possibly could. Terray encouraged us in this. From past lecturing tours in France he knew what an attraction a good climbing film makes. On films taken by most expeditions one is apt to get far too

many shots of camp scenes, rarely pictures of actual hard climbing at great height.

De Booy, poor fellow, always got the worst end of the stick in this connection. As last man on the rope, he was charged with the responsibility for camera work—no sinecure, believe you me, in that rarefied atmosphere. When taking photographs one is supposed to hold one's breath as much as possible. Time and time again I used to hear De Booy cursing under his breath as a 'start filming' yell came down to him from Terray. Although De Booy swore at the time, it was thanks to Terray that we finished up with a truly fine colour film of the ascent.

My climb up the ice-wall was filmed, too. Although, of course, I didn't do it with such dash and style as Terray, at least, I did not cut the comic figure of the day before, when, at the north summit, I showed how things 'should *not* be done'.

Above the ice-wall the ridge was still steep. Sitting astride the crest, secured by a rammed-in axe, I had a brief opportunity to look around. On both sides there were sheer intimidating drops. From this extremely airy perch the most striking thing was how all the other mountains round about suddenly seemed to have dwindled to small and insignificant proportions. Even the Cayesh lost much of its terrifying appearance and looked more like a sharp pinnacle rising on some far-off ridge. The wind had died down. It was ideal weather: a clear blue sky with just a few cloud banks far away on the distant horizon.

We followed the ridge up for a few more rope lengths, then the eternal cornice started spoiling the game. Huge masses of ice hung over the west face. From now on we had to avoid the crest and seek a way along the east flank of the mountain, where deep powdery snow made the going difficult. The summit was no longer visible, but it couldn't be far away. As our bodies tired, so our nerves became tauter. Time after time we found our upward path barred by these poised masses of ice. Each time Terray managed to wangle a

way out of the impasse, by traversing further along the face. On one occasion this involved climbing a small but almost perpendicular ice-wall, into which handholds and footholds had to be cut.

Suddenly the summit came into sight again. The worst was over! We knew now that, despite all the difficulties, victory could not escape us. I called down to De Booy that another half-hour would see us there; but he—usually the irrepressible optimist—called back somewhat curtly: 'Keep quiet! I'll believe it only when I'm there.'

It certainly did sound almost too good to be true. We went on and on. Hitherto, our goal had seemed interminably far away, but now, after all these weeks of effort, there it was for the taking! Terray forged ahead. Three or four rope lengths more up the steep wall! One last section of the ridge! And 'J'Y SUIS!' Terray was there!

Five minutes later, at one o'clock in the afternoon of July 7th, we all shook hands. The proud, inviolate summit of the Huantsán, the 20,981-ft. fastness, had fallen.

Victory was ours!

We still felt all on edge however. Perhaps the American expedition, which also had ambitions on the Huantsán, had forestalled us? But they had left no traces either on the summit or on the lower portions of the mountain. The top was still virgin! We stood on untrodden ground! After a siege of more than three weeks, the mighty fortress of snow and ice had at length capitulated. Beneath our feet lay the highest unconquered peak in the whole of the Cordillera Blanca, the mountain which tradition had said was unclimbable. We could just make out the tiny tents of our base camp on the edge of the lake more than 6,500 feet below. So incredibly far away that it looked remotely unreal. We waved our arms on the off-chance that the bearers down there might be looking up through the field-glasses.

Terray wanted to leave some concrete proof that we had been on the summit, something that could be seen from far-off Huaraz,

a little town just visible to the west, down the valley. Accordingly, out of the cornice he hacked an enormous piece which fell with an unholy noise into the abyss. We talked about the Americans and speculated as to what we should have done had they, in fact, been there before us. Back in Holland it had, of course, been easy enough to write in lofty vein, saying that it was the climbing of the mountain that mattered and that it was really quite unimportant which party first reached the top. But now that we actually were the first, we would hardly have been human if our success had not given us a feeling of great exhilaration.

We had a feeling of being high above the world, of floating in space, of not belonging to this earth. Each of us experienced something of this sort in his own individual way. I, myself, cannot remember ever succumbing to a sensation like that before. It was a feeling that permeated slowly and was perhaps, because of that, all the more intense.

For me, this moment saw the fulfilment of a dream, a dream which went back years, long before I had ever heard of the Huantsán. The campaign of the past few weeks with the mountain had become of vital importance. I was naturally thankful that the attempt had been crowned with success, and that I had been able to participate personally in the final victory. Yet I realized, even at that moment, that unconditional readiness to devote one's whole self to the struggle was, after all, the main thing. Sitting up there in that glittering white world, with the two friends who had shared these past exciting, eventful weeks, I knew that this was definitely, in every sense, a high spot in my life, something of permanent value.

The way in which De Booy's mind was working was not difficult to guess. One had only to look at his sparkling eyes. They revealed his innermost thoughts. He was much younger than I, and had many other climbing ambitions. He would undoubtedly go on to more successes in the future, successes which would perhaps take

him even higher than the Huantsán. But it was doubtful if he would ever get a greater thrill than now, from this decisive combat with his first big mountain.

As far as Terray was concerned, the victory was just one more in the long series of resounding successes which had marked his career. The elation now filling De Booy and me for the first time, was nothing new to him. All the same, one could tell that he, too, was highly pleased with the result. And who had more right to be jubilant? But for his inspiring leadership we should never have reached this height.

It was Terray, typically, who put an end to all our musings by remarking: 'Now if a voice behind me suddenly said: 'Hi, Terray, what on earth are you doing up here?' I should jump right out of my skin!' We all burst out laughing. The mere thought of an acquaintance turning up here, on this giant peak, with such a nonchalant greeting, really tickled us.

My thoughts turned to the things to come, the difficulties to be faced during the descent, the days we should still have to spend on the mountain. Actually it was a little presumptuous to boast of victory in view of the long, long way down to earth, the ridge stretching nearly two miles and bristling with obstacles. Talk of success ought to be deferred until we had left the mountain well and truly behind.

Anyhow, we allowed ourselves time to have something to eat and drink. I unearthed from my rucksack a tin of meat which we had kept back specially for this occasion. But none of us now fancied it. The only things which did not revolt us at that high altitude were Verkade's gingerbread and a drink of lemon water. We took the usual photographs of our two national flags, fastened to axes.

THE DESCENT

After half an hour on the summit Terray gave the sign for departure. De Booy took the lead in going down the steep slope. I, myself, have never relished descending steep ice, and I had to force myself to keep pace with the others. Terray kept egging me on. He was anxious not to be caught by night on the ridge and he simply would not tolerate any going slow on the simpler passages. But, as it happened, the various complications which had so bothered us that morning were now taken in our stride, even the vertical ice-wall. Nerves were decidedly better. Compared with that morning, everything seemed very much easier. The big worry of every 'first' ascent is, of course, not knowing precisely what lies ahead.

Once back on the *arête* the descent accelerated. At the iced-up section we drove in a piton and slid swiftly down the rope. Carefully negotiating the steep slope below, we crossed the crest on to the west face and at 4.30 arrived back in Camp 4. The first part of the descent was over!

It was still lovely weather. Our first job in camp was a thorough foot inspection. Terray's feet, so bad that morning, were now found happily to be quite in order. De Booy had small blue spots at the ends of his toes. As circulation gradually returned during the coming night he was to become acutely aware of those spots. My feet were worst off. Not only were there inky spots in my foot pads at one or two places, but the outsides of my big toes were more or less dead. De Booy and Terray took my feet masterfully in hand. They rubbed and rubbed away until at last feeling gradually returned.

It was a beautiful evening. Mists were rolling up the east face from the valley below, and the last glowing rays of the sun tinged the fantastic north summit, half-hidden in cloud, with fairy-like

tints. To us the evening was all the more wonderful because of the great day that now lay behind and the promise the benign heavens gave of an easy trip next day.

While Terray filmed the marvellous sunset, I devoted my time to stewing prunes and apricots. The tinned fruits were now all gone. Somehow we did not hanker after any other form of food. Actually, we had been living for days on our bodily reserves, and counted ourselves lucky that our past years of rigorous training had built them up so abundantly. We were now so well acclimatized that we were able to get a good night's sleep. A pill or two helped maybe.

Next morning we stayed extra long in our sleeping-bags. There was no need to rush, for it was impossible to get down as far as Camp 2 in one day and, in view of the prepared track, it ought to be just a pleasant saunter to the site of Camp 3, which was located above the north-west ridge.

Leaving, the only difficulty we did encounter was the ice-wall on the way up the north summit; but once over that summit the route led down over simple terrain. In fact, I could hardly bring myself to believe that this selfsame section had involved such a terrific struggle two days before. Probably it was a matter of acclimatization.

Then, when we came to the small plateau above the ridge, Terray allowed us, as a great exception to his usual rule, a full hour's rest. Relaxing to the full, we feasted our eyes for the last time on the Huantsán summit ridge. Now that the nervous strain was over we glibly started making all sorts of speculations about various incidents that had occurred, wondering what would have happened if . . . ?

Towards three in the afternoon we reached the site of Camp 3, and for the first time during the whole climb we did not have to rush to set up a tent. We did it lazily. And once done, we leisurely stretched our limbs on the mattresses and basked blissfully in the warm sun.

An hour before dusk, De Booy and Terray went along to have a

The descent: Terray prepares to go down *en rappel* over a projecting wall of ice

look at the upper part of the north-west ridge. Terray had decided to go down the first steep section by means of a long rappel, and he wanted to make certain preparations with a view to saving time next day.

As usual, I took the cooking in hand. There was no need for me to scratch my head puzzledly over a choice of viands, because there was very little left. All I had to prepare was mashed potatoes. That would be followed by stewed plums. The small quantity of rice that still remained would have to be kept for next day.

Whilst I was engrossed with the spirit stoves the sun suddenly went behind the clouds and, startled, I noticed that the mountain had become completely shrouded in mist. A little later it began to snow softly. Did this portend a change in the weather? That would be a rotten stroke of luck with the long and dangerous trip down the north-west ridge in prospect. On climbing it, the difficulties inherent in this *arête* had impressed me sharply, and in the past few days uneasy thoughts about its trying complications had kept coming up in my mind. I knew that my companions regarded it dubiously, too, although no mention was ever made of it. We all avoided giving expression to our qualms. All three of us fully realized though how bad weather conditions could jeopardize our operations. In fact, it was no good beating about the bush—if the weather changed seriously for the worse, there we were, caught like rats in a trap in Camp 3 with hardly any food or cooking spirit.

But anyone attempting a climb in a high range such as the Cordillera Blanca simply has to face up to the fact that chances *have* to be taken; otherwise one might as well stop at home. The greatest risk in climbing the Huantsán was undoubtedly the length of time required for the ascent. And during this extended time one needed a period of settled good weather. The north-west ridge was the first full-scale technical problem set by the mountain. It was, indeed, the most dangerous part of the whole climb. If the weather changed during an attempt and the assault had to be abandoned,

there was no possible way of avoiding a return down this most un-compromising section.

But why meet trouble half-way? Up to now we had always managed to scrape through. When Terray and De Booy returned to Camp 3 night had already fallen. Not a word was uttered about the weather. None of us wished to voice our general uneasiness, nevertheless a certain degree of apprehension hung in the air, and it was with mixed feelings that we turned in for the night. We in-dulged in a form of escapism. Instead of sleeping, we talked far into the night about this, that, and the other thing—of the mountains we hoped to climb in the future. It was the same old story: one climb not even over before our minds were occupied with thoughts of other more ambitious projects..

When morning came, fate—for the n'th time—was kind. One glance outside sufficed to dispel all our nervous fears. The morning was perfect. The sky was cloudless, and—for the first time that week—the wind had dropped. Our final trial of strength with the Huantsán was going to take place, thank goodness, under favour-able weather conditions! We felt considerably relieved. Whilst packing up, we optimistically planned to reach Camp 2 early and then, like conquering lords of creation, go jauntily on, enjoying the midday sun, down to base camp.

About eight o'clock we broke camp, cast one last look at the im-pressive north-west face of the south summit, and then set off. Later on, in the course of our geological work, we might get another look at it, but not of course at such close quarters and never so ideally as now. Crossing the sloping plateau, we went down to the place where Terray had prepared the first rappel.

Here we had to make the first 200-ft. rope descent down the steep face. Terray had been elated the night before about the result of his work, and he now proudly exhibited his *champignon de glace*. Where the ridge was steepest he had cut, in the crest itself, a wide shelf on which all three of us could comfortably stand. In the middle

of this tiny plateau he had hewn out an artificial mushroom—a mound of ice about a foot in diameter. And he had looped a rope-sling in a groove running round it, using some old paper as packing to prevent the sling-cord cutting too deeply into the far side of the mushroom. By pulling our long ropes through the sling, a descent of a cool 200 feet became possible. Terray was as happy as a sandboy when De Booy and I came out with exclamations of wonder. This put him in an exceptionally good temper. Except for his dark stubbly beard no one would have guessed that he had been working at such top pressure for five whole days.

Though most of the preparatory work had been done the day before, it was quite a time before De Booy, as first, went down the steep wall. Whilst I tensely watched his every move from my exposed position, my feet—which had been cold ever since we left camp—suddenly felt dead, probably due to lack of movement. The bright calm weather tended to make one overlook how terribly cold it was. I debated with Terray what to do. He had an awesome fear of frost-bite and would gladly have taken my boots off there and then, but on that steep incline it was quite impossible. Hoping that movement might help to restore circulation, I went down the rope and was quickly followed by Terray. There was no place to sit. The ridge was too steep and had, moreover, a dangerous cornice. There was nothing for it but to go on doggedly down until a level spot was reached. But, alas, before we found one, more than an hour had gone by, and even then it was just a ledge and I was the only one able to sit down. My two friends were perched around me in the most awkward of positions. Off came my rucksack! It had to be secured to a well-driven-in axe. Then off came my boots. They also had to be well secured. The mere thought of their so easily vanishing into the abyss below made one quake.

With socks removed, one could see that the front halves of my feet had gone white. The toes were devoid of feeling. De Booy and Terray each took charge of a foot. They began massaging and beat-

ing my feet with the rope until, slowly but surely, feeling returned. But thirty minutes of their hard-handed treatment brought me to the stage of writhing with pain. Terray had massaged my feet before at night times and I therefore knew the extraordinary strength that lay in his fingers. It seemed now as though he were going all out to rub the skin right off. My remonstrances had some effect on De Booy, but all the curses I hurled at Terray's head only evoked: 'It's hellish painful, I know—but it's *got* to be done!'

And then he went at it harder than ever. The most stubborn dead spot was on the side of my big toe. Although the rest of my foot had now become warm, mainly because Terray had put it under his vest against his own naked chest, this particular spot remained obstinately frozen. As a kill or cure measure Terray finally took the big toe in his mouth and chewed it as hard as he could. He gnawed and bit, until I was curling up in agony. Then, and only then, did he desist. The pain indicated to his satisfaction that the blood had begun to flow again. Socks, boots, and crampons were put on, rucksack donned, and the descent was renewed as quickly as possible.

But the delay meant that our wishful early picnic return to Camp 2 could not possibly come off. We could see the two small tents below, looking deceptively close. But our downward progress towards them was extremely slow, for the lower we got, the more menacing became the cornice peril, and time after time we were forced to traverse on to the steep flank of the *arête*. The sun was stronger, too, making snow conditions less favourable, so the greatest care had to be exercised. Yet Terray kept urging us to keep up speed. Once he said:

'Don't be afraid to put a move on, Kees! If you fall, I shall be there—to hold you on the rope!'

But for me this went right against the grain. Two years before, towards the end of a long tiring climb in the mountains near Chamonix, the pace had been forced somewhat beyond my power to maintain. In order to gain time I had gone, at Terray's insistence,

over my limit while descending the Whymper couloir of the Aiguille Verte. As a result I slipped several times and, on one occasion, only the rope saved me from a headlong plunge into the depths. The strain had been so severe that I had vowed never to let it happen again if I could possibly help it. At Chamonix it was a case of full speed ahead in order to avoid the necessity of a bivouac. But there was no threat of that at this juncture on the Huantsán.

I had another reason, too, for holding back. The Huantsán was our mountain, the lofty peak which the three of us had climbed as a team and yet which, in a manner of speaking, was the treasured property of each of us individually. In that sense it was 'my' mountain: probably the greatest and most ambitious that I would ever master. And it was for that reason that I wanted to tackle everything myself. I wanted to do it all, if possible, under my own power. There was no immediate threat of a bivouac, so I felt perfectly justified in carrying on to the best of my ability. If it meant arriving at Camp 2 a little later—well, we should have to arrive a little later, and that was all there was to it.

Discretion warned me, of course, not to mention this to Terray. Neither did I deem it necessary to voice any sneaking doubts I might have about his really being able to hold me if I fell, situated as he was in a most delicate position on the steep ice-wall. There were the unsatisfactory snow conditions to take into account, too. No, I wasn't going to risk anything!

At three, when we reached a point about 500 feet directly above the camp, Terray suddenly had an inspiration. He distinctly remembered the dangers of the parts of the ridge still below us and how, at the time of ascent, we had somewhat grimly pointed out to one another that this lower section was not going to be a birthday treat on the return journey, for it was not possible to circumvent the treacherous cornice all the time. Terray had obviously been debating in his mind for some time whether it would be possible to get down the east flank by a series of rappels. When, yet once again, we came

up against massive overhanging snow and ice, round which we saw no means of detouring but would have to risk negotiating, Terray turned and asked me to secure him extra well. Then he started to go down the snow-covered slope. About a hundred feet down he sought a suitable place from which to engineer a rappel. But driving in a piton gave no security in that deep powdery snow. He dug deeply with his axe, trying to reach ice, but without success. This meant that it would be impossible to make an ice-mushroom as he had done higher up the ridge. De Booy and I, indeed, saw no alternative but to ram in one of the axes and to use that as a sort of big piton. The objection was, of course, that the axe would afterwards have to be written off as lost for good.

De Booy and I looked dubiously at each other. The uncertainty made us somewhat uneasy. But the indomitable Terray had more than one string to his bow. He dug an enormous circular channel in the snow, rather like the one he had hacked out the night before: but this time nearly five feet in diameter, instead of one. His new creation was no less than a gigantic mushroom of snow, which could be used however in precisely the same way as the ice-mushroom. A sling was put round and Lionel tugged at it with all his might to see whether it would hold. It seemed safe enough, save that the thin cord of the sling cut deeply into the upper side of the mushroom. To stop this, my spare gloves were sacrificed to serve as packing between rope and snow. Then, at last, Terray was satisfied.

Making the snow mushroom had taken over half an hour, during which time De Booy and I had necessarily to remain practically motionless on the unpleasantly steep face. We gradually felt the tedium, that we had had more than enough of it all. Now that we were, so to speak, so close to 'home'—after these six days of intensive effort—it was going to be difficult at this last stage to muster up the concentration needed for this tricky manœuvre.

For the first time during the whole attack a feeling of disquiet

crept over me. Supposing that blessed mushroom gave way? Up to now I had been ready to take any justifiable risk to reach our goal. But now, when the great adventure was practically over, my readiness somehow waned. Thinking it over later on, I came to the conclusion that it was precisely at this moment that the everyday world, with all its ties, big and small, crowded back on me. The bond with the mountain had broken. The Huantsán dream had ended. We had reached the summit, had overcome innumerable difficulties. Now I longed only to get back safe and sound, to be able to tell them at home about our mountain and about the happenings up there. And, more than anything, I longed for fresh mountains to tackle.

I was not the only one thinking along those lines apparently. For the first time during the assault my partners also showed signs of jumpiness. At one time Terray and De Booy even had a brisk exchange of words about some manœuvre or other that De Booy was alleged to have messed up. I grinned at De Booy and remarked in Dutch: 'Isn't all this sickening!'

And he answered, in all honesty: 'I'm fed up to the teeth!'

So he felt that way, too! What a comforting discovery! I had felt rather ashamed of my own pusillanimity, but now that my friend appeared to be going through a similar phase, I bucked up straightaway. And so did he. We both suddenly burst out laughing, and with renewed spirit girded up our loins for the last decisive effort.

The mushroom finished, De Booy slid down first. At the end of the rope, 200 feet below, he hacked out a roomy step in the wall. I followed while Terray kept an anxious eye on the mushroom. But it stood up to my weight all right. Ten minutes later Terray himself was down and immediately set about making a second mushroom. When it was ready there came another sort of hitch. We discovered that we had insufficient rope to make the sling to go round the mushroom. We had been using a special nylon cord or line of 5 mm thickness for making these slings and we had used up over 80

ack in base camp:

Top: Egeler sees to the inner man
Left: Terray sees to the cooking
Right: De Booy sees to his toilet

feet of it on the Huantsán. The inventive De Booy suddenly hit on the idea of using the cord from his hammer for the purpose. Saved again!

Then came the last critical moment. The ice-wall ended down below in a bulge which overhung the bergschrund, the crevasse separating the glacier from the mountain. Would the rappel be long enough to reach the 'underlip' of the bergschrund? Only when De Booy had actually descended to the brink and was able to peer over the edge, could he set our minds at rest as to the position down there. Yes, the length of double-rope was more than sufficient! He vanished over the bulge, remained out of sight a while, and then we saw him, safe and sound, down on the gently-inclined glacier.

I followed as smartly as possible. A longing for the moment of deliverance from the mountain possessed me, the moment when we could say the descent was well and truly behind us. Reaching the overhang, I let my legs dangle in space and took a quick glance down. Only 16 feet separated me from the glacier. For the last time I hung weightily on the rope, lowering myself laboriously down from the overhang. Phew! Plumping into the snow, I sighed with relief. The Huantsán was definitely now a thing of the past.

In the course of this last passage I had hurt my hand. De Booy hastily applied a first-aid dressing; then we filmed Terray negotiating the overhang and dangling through the air over the bergschrund.

Five minutes later we came to Camp 2. Everything was still intact. We looked forward to a good meal, to mopping up lovely big chunks of cake, tinned fruits and other tasty delicacies. All that afternoon we had been thinking of nothing else, for the lower we came, the more sharply our appetites revived.

I dived into the tents and brought out everything. What a disappointment! How mistaken we were about the stores left behind five days ago! To satisfy our keen gastronomic desires, to appease that gnawing inner man, there were no more than a couple of

The Huantsán seen from the south-east

miserable tins of semi-frozen vegetables. We had awful thirsts, too; but could not melt any snow as there was no more spirit for the stove.

Now that the acute problems of the day lay behind us, now that the strain and stress were over, we felt an urgent need of comfort. Camp 2 offered precious little in this respect.

Someone—I forget who—suggested getting down to base camp that same day. It was hard to say what attracted and lured us most—the prospect of a good meal: the comparative comfort of air-mattresses, tables, and chairs; the luxury of being waited upon; *or* news from home? Blasido by now would have fetched the post from Ticapampa, and letters would be awaiting our arrival down below. The temptations were too great, we did not delay another second. Half-past five saw us in motion again, rapidly descending the glacier, and then later on climbing a little again to reach the gully. We even had the energy and inclination to do a little geological investigation of some interesting rock near the gully, for we knew that we should not be returning that way again.

With the Huantsán campaign ended, the other side of our mission imperceptibly slipped into its proper place. For days on end all that had mattered was getting up to that summit and then coming safely down again. All thought of our scientific work had been driven to the background, but now it got into focus once more as the main objective of our expedition. We used the last minutes of daylight in geological work. Even Terray, who was no geologist, was fired by our enthusiasm and nobly helped by climbing up and procuring a sample or two from a difficult high position. It came to light later, in the course of the laboratory examinations, that the fieldwork put in on that particular evening was of considerable value.

In the gathering dusk the Huantsán once more revealed itself to us in all its majestic grandeur. It was as if the mighty mountain had concluded a pact of eternal friendship with us, and now wished us

to take away an unforgettable picture of it at its best. Violet shadows glided slowly across the snow-covered slopes. Even when the valley below and the lower reaches of the mountain itself were shrouded in gloom, the last lingering rays of the tropical sun caressingly haloed the south summit, until this, too, softly faded into the night.

Silently, in increasing dark, we followed the track we had made six days before, each of us wrapped in thought. So much had happened in the last few days. It was difficult to realize that the great adventure was over. Every step took us further from the mountain to which we had devoted six whole days of supreme effort, this mountain which had so fiercely beaten off our first attempts, but which had latterly done everything in its power to smooth our path to its crown, as though it had resigned itself eventually to the inevitable and cherished no ill will at its conquest.

It was remarkable how quickly we adjusted ourselves to the changed circumstances. My thoughts strayed to the days ahead. My toes were hurting abominably. I hoped the frost-bite would not prove a handicap on our further geological fieldwork. I felt that my big toes, though they had thawed out to a great extent that morning, were beginning to go dead again.

Before negotiating the steeper part of the glacier we rested for a few minutes, took our torches from the rucksacks, and then proceeded down quickly until we reached the ice-fall. There, for the last time, we laced on our crampons. As we went warily through the narrow gully below the séracs, we heard a great avalanche come thundering down the east face of the Huantsán. It was the mountain bidding us *farewell*.

After that, everything seemed wonderfully still. The silence was deep. Beneath a sky filled with glittering stars we made our way lower and lower. It all seemed ethereally unreal. Reaching the moraine, we picked our way in the darkness as well as we could, zigzagging through the great boulders. Then followed a fifteen minutes' climb which we took in our stride. Excitement set in. We

were now full of the thrill of return: news from home; a drink of water to slake our terrible thirsts; creature comforts generally. Our recall to earth was complete.

At 8.30 we reached base camp to be greated with uproarious joy by the porters. It did us good to see how unfeignedly glad they were about our success, especially Guillermo. He was perhaps the only one of them who really understood all that this climb had meant to us. While Blasido and Leucadio got on with the preparations for a festive meal, we literally fell on our masses of mail.

There was a pile of letters for each of us. I myself had a round dozen, including no less than seven from my wife. In addition, there was a ten-day-old cable from her, notifying me that there was actually the chance of a house becoming available in Amsterdam and asking me to let her know promptly if it would be all right for her to proceed with the purchase. My word, we were back to civilization indeed!

There was so much to wade through that I hardly knew where to begin. By the flickering light of a candle I read for over an hour and a half without stopping. It was the same with the others. Within thirty minutes of our arrival the porters served up a meal, a splendid repast: beef and fried potatoes, followed by our favourite mixed fruits. But we were all so engrossed in our reading matter that we gave ourselves no time to enjoy it as it deserved, but merely guzzled it in a most inattentive manner.

Again and again we excitedly exchanged titbits from our letters. There were press cuttings from France and Holland, commenting on our Pongos victory. It was a wonderful evening. We all felt just a little intoxicated with the magic of it. So deep was I in my reading that Terray later had to force my down-jacket on me. It was one o'clock in the morning before everything had been read, all the news exchanged, and everything discussed. Then, at long last, we crept into our sleeping-bags and snuffed out the candles. But sleep did not come easily. There had been too much to digest that even-

ing, and I lay awake for hours, turning this and that over in my mind.

When about three I finally dropped off, my last thought was one of great thankfulness. 'What a life!' I said to myself. 'I've not only been on top of the Huantsán, but I've also the chance to buy a house—which, considering the housing problem in Holland, is a very remarkable thing. First thing to-morrow I must see about sending off a cable telling my wife to buy that house right away!'

Then I sank into a deep, dreamless sleep.

DEPARTURE

The sun was already high in the sky before we awoke on the morning after our return to base camp. Now that we were no longer above the 16,000-ft. level we had been able to sleep much better. Having had no trouble with my feet during the night, I got up cheerfully and tried to stand as usual, but immediately found that my big toes were inflamed and swollen. Walking was very painful. Thank goodness there was no longer any need to struggle with those tight-fitting mountaineering boots. As the day was to be devoted to rest I wore a pair of comfortable-fitting camp boots lined with lamb's wool.

De Booy took stock of the food position. The number of tins had dwindled alarmingly, so it was high time to return to the civilized world. In any case, why remain here? There was no more to do. Our summit had been reached and base camp no longer served any useful purpose.

After a discussion we agreed to depart early the next day. As we were not doing anything particular that day, we had time to spare to have a quiet talk with the porters about the past few days. We were curious to hear how they had fared at base whilst we were

up on the mountain. We also wanted to know to what degree they had interested themselves in our climb.

Blasido had been away most of the time down the valley. He had gone as far as Ticapampa to collect the post. Guillermo and Leucadio had remained the whole time in the vicinity of the camp. It transpired that they had scaled a near-by height on various occasions and followed our progress through field-glasses. On the morning of July 7th they had managed to spot us about 150 feet below the summit of the Huantsán. On the preceding days they had, of course, been unable to see anything of us, as Camp 4, sited on the saddle between the north and south summits, was hidden from their view.

Guillermo had undoubtedly been with us in spirit. As he told of the moment when we came within focus up there, close to the summit, his eyes shone. 'Ah, Señor!' he exclaimed, 'That was great! That was something I shall never forget!' He, too, apparently was now infected by the virus of alpinism. We promised that we should certainly send for him, if ever we came back to the Andes.

Guillermo recounted an intriguing story. It was a common local belief that during the intoxication induced by the chewing of the coca leaf one was sometimes vouchsafed the gift of looking into the future. He said that Leucadio had been chewing these coca leaves on various occasions during the past week in order to find out what our chances were of reaching the top. His powers of clairvoyance must have been pathetically low. According to Leucadio, we did not stand a dog's chance of success with the mountain. On the contrary, he foresaw the whole affair turning out very badly for us indeed. But what tickled us most of all was the fact that it was Guillermo who, prompted by his anxiety to know how we were getting on, kept urging Leucadio to chew the coca leaf. He himself could not indulge in the habit, as it was against his religious beliefs.

Continuing the conversations, we were once again struck forcibly by the fact that these natives had simply no idea whatsoever of

the great distances to be covered up there, not a clue as to the enormous technical difficulties to be overcome at those great heights. Leucadio, for instance, on looking through the glasses and seeing us so close to the summit that midday, calmly remarked: 'They'll be back here to-night—or, at the latest, to-morrow night!'

It was only when time went on and on, without sight of us, that the bearers began to get worried. In fact, they had decided—just before we suddenly turned up late that night in base camp—that next day they would all go up to Camp 2.

It was necessary to draw up some plan of action for the next few days. The condition of my feet rendered it impossible for me to make the long journey to Chavin on foot. Luckily Blasido had his mule at the camp. It was decided that I should ride this down the valley next day, whilst De Booy and Terray followed on foot. If they put best foot forward we might all reach Chavin the same day. Then, while the three of us carried on to Ticapampa, Blasido could return to base camp—with the same *arriero* who had accompanied us on the way up—in order to break camp and bring everything down the valley. During our absence Leucadio would remain in camp to keep an eye on things.

Early next morning it was with a feeling akin to melancholy that I turned my back for the last time on base camp. I had become quite attached to this sunny little spot beside the lake. It had become a part of my life, a place never to be forgotten.

Guillermo came with Blasido and me, as his services were no longer required in base camp. When I saw Blasido carrying a sack-full of empty tins on his back I asked what on earth he was going to do with them. Both he and Guillermo burst out laughing. Blasido himself would not say anything, but Guillermo could not suppress the news for long. Still cackling with merriment, he said: 'Ah, Señor Doctor, eso es para una mujer!' (They're for a woman!) All this went over my head at first. I idly wondered whether

Blasido was taking the tins home to his wife. A few hours later we neared the first settlement of huts and when Guillermo began broadly grinning again, a light began to dawn on me. My dark suspicions were shortly confirmed on seeing Blasido sidle up to a hut and being warmly greeted by a peasant woman. On his way to and from Ticapampa a little while back he had, of course, passed this little settlement and the 'tender' friendship then struck up was now being cemented by this gift of empty tins.

The uses made of those tins! Wherever we went during our trips all sorts of services were willingly offered us in return for empty tins. The people in the mountain districts obviously found them useful in all sorts of ways, as pans, drinking vessels, etc.

The way down, enlivened though it was by this incident, was long. Yet I did not find it at all monotonous. The scenery was magnificent and I had more than enough to occupy my thoughts. Halfway through the afternoon I called a halt at the end of the Carhuascancha valley. From there I sent Guillermo off to San Marcos with that long-overdue cable to my wife. She had already been kept in suspense far too long. Wanting to send her all the news in one go, I concocted what must have been one of the most peculiarly assorted telegrams of all time. It not only announced our conquest of the Huantsán, but was also a wedding anniversary greeting, and ended by telling her to buy that long-desired house in Amsterdam.

It was dark when Blasido and I at last entered Chavin, and at first the place seemed entirely deserted. But in a couple of minutes people were thronging round us in the market-place. They wanted to know what had happened. Had we actually reached the summit? Why were my friends not with me? Had they met with mishap?

As well as my halting Spanish would allow I told them about our adventures, my tale being continually punctuated by the 'Oh's' and 'Ah's' of the crowd. They simply could not understand why we had been away so long. The police officer who had taken our names and addresses on the previous occasion, also turned up, excessively

Top: Blasido and Guillermo.   *Bottom:* Eugenio and Pelegrino

polite as usual. He expressed his gratification that our climb had been crowned with success.

When at last everything had been told, the crowd gradually dispersed and I went along to the little café where we had had such a beano on our previous visit. We had promised if we ever reached that summit to hold a fiesta there by way of celebration. So it was a big disappointment when they saw I was alone. All the same I was given a hearty welcome; and the food was fine.

Time went by, and I could not understand why Terray and De Booy had not put in an appearance. At ten o'clock I stretched my weary limbs in my sleeping-bag in the middle of the market-place, feeling positively too tired and sleepy to worry about anything. About four o'clock in the morning the noise of a lorry pulling up close by awoke me. It was De Booy. Terray and he had reached San Marcos the previous evening, but had been too dog-tired to plod on to Chavin. They had bivouacked in the San Marcos market-place until they had been able to get a lift in a lorry. As it was bound for the Santa valley Terray now went on down in it.

Next morning De Booy and I laid on arrangements whereby Guillermo and Leucadio could get our stores transported from Chavin during the next few days. We ourselves, about noon, were lucky enough to get a lift in a lorry going to Ticapampa. And so it was that five o'clock saw us entering the garden of our genial host, Mr. Kroupnitzky. He was standing just outside the house, talking to a friend, and at first he looked at us blankly. It was not surprising. Our bearded faces, tanned skins, and grubby appearance generally, must have rendered us unrecognizable to anyone who had not witnessed the metamorphosis from day to day. But curiouser and curiouser! On going into the house we ourselves were surprised to see a very smart-looking stranger sitting there in an armchair, reading by the fireside. Now it was our turn to be slow to recognize. But then, a trim, clean-shaven Terray was someone we hardly remembered.

173

The steepest mountain in the whole Cordillera Blanca, the Cayesh (18,770 feet)

Our safe return to Ticapampa concluded the climbing part of our Andes expedition. Hopes we had fondly cherished of being able, perhaps, to make a quick attempt on some other peak were dashed, alas, by Lionel Terray's inability to stay much longer in Perú. We did plan to go together for a few days to the northerly part of the Santa valley and have a look at the mountains there. But nothing came of that either, because two days after our return to Ticapampa who should fall a victim to a bad attack of influenza, but Terray himself.

I was not in any good shape either. Both my big toes were painfully swollen and, on medical advice, I had to rest up as much as possible. Perhaps this was all for the best, for there was an ever-increasing correspondence relating to our Andes expedition to be answered. News of our success had reached Holland and France, and masses of mail now came flooding in. The Executive Committee of the Royal Netherlands Alpine Club sent a congratulatory cable. There were letters galore from our families, friends, and interested parties.

During a visit to the township of Huaraz, De Booy and I were the guests of a Peruvian mountaineering club—the 'Grupo Andinista Cordillera Blanca', and to celebrate our success, a lunch was held at the residence of the Morales family. It was during the course of this festive occasion that we were formally installed as honorary members of the Grupo. The renown of Lionel Terray was, of course, fully appreciated in Huaraz, and it was a bitter disappointment to everyone that illness prevented this great Alpinist—and now also *Andinist*—from being present.

Several days after our trip to Huaraz two members of the group paid a visit to Ticapampa. Though Terray was on the mend, he still had to stay in bed. Our worthy Peruvian friends pleaded so hard to have just a glimpse of the great man that, to Lionel's consternation, we obligingly ushered them into the sick room. To his utter horror, they photographed the heroic Terray *in bed*. Never, during the

whole expedition, did we see him look so confused and embarrassed as then.

On July 16th came the day of his departure. It was an emaciated Lionel to whom we said good-bye. We were sorry indeed to see him go. During the past few weeks he had come to mean so much more to us than a first-class mountain-climber. A strong feeling of affection now bound us together.

Just before he stepped into the car taking him to Lima, Terray said to us: 'Don't forget, whatever happens, I'm coming with you on the next expedition. We've scored some good technical successes out here; but, for me, it is still more important to find a good friend for life. During this expedition I reckon to have found two. If only because of that, this venture will always stay in my memory.'

And so, with Terray's departure, came the definite close to the climbing part of our expedition. Behind us lay unforgettable experiences. We had fought a battle of life and death to gain the summit of an unconquered world-mountain. We had tackled it, each in his own individual way; but all three of us had striven to the fullest limits of our physical and spiritual capacities to reach our fixed objective. Luck had been with us—an enormous amount of luck. And . . . we had experienced the satisfaction of winning through to victory.

RETROSPECT

On weighing up the results of the mountaineering side of our Andes expedition we cannot help feeling highly satisfied. The ascent of the Pongos and especially the climb to the Huantsán summit were exploits we had hardly dared hope to achieve. We owed much of our success on these climbs first and foremost to big slices of luck. Fate was indeed kind to us. And naturally good team-work also played an important role. Another vital factor was the judicious period of acclimatization without which the two Dutch participants at least could not possibly have managed the climbs.

Due prominence has been given in previous pages to our 'lucky' breaks on various occasions, as well as to our excellent mutual relationships. Here it is desired to say something about acclimatization and all that it entails.

The attuning of the human body to the vastly different conditions prevailing at high altitudes is an important feature of any stay in a high mountainous region such as the Cordillera Blanca. Much has been written in the last few decades on this subject, chiefly by doctors connected with expeditions to the Himalayas or Andes, who made all sorts of tests and kept careful note of the reactions of themselves and their colleagues during sojourns at great heights.

It is an acknowledged fact that the air contains less oxygen at high altitudes than at sea-level. True, the proportions of oxygen and nitrogen remain constant; but the barometric pressure of the atmospheric gases steadily decreases the higher one goes. This means that

the actual amount of oxygen taken in at each breath and absorbed, via the lungs, into the blood-stream is far less than normal. As a consequence a diminished supply of oxygen is conveyed to the tissues. It is this which evokes attacks of mountain-sickness, and it is to meet this deficiency of oxygen that the body has to adapt itself, by the process commonly termed 'Acclimatization'.

There are a variety of symptoms of mountain-sickness, the most common being breathlessness, dizziness, headaches, and nausea—the last sometimes provoking actual vomiting. The dire effects of mountain-sickness are felt most acutely when ascent to high altitudes takes place too rapidly to give the body time to adapt itself, even if only partially. Acclimatization is a slow, gradual process; in fact it may take weeks to become really effective. It is, of course, nothing but a marshalling of the body's powers of resistance to combat the effect of the insufficiency of oxygen. Increase of pulmonary ventilation plays an important part in this connection, whilst another reaction is for the body to increase the number of red corpuscles, whose function it is to convey oxygen to the system generally.

Although the human body can adapt itself to a limited extent and for limited periods to conditions at very high altitudes, it is not capable of standing up to the strain for any considerable length of time. Argyll-Campbell and Sir Leonard Hill made experiments with animals to see how long they could exist under low atmospheric pressure. The results made it clear that no useful purpose could possibly be served by remaining any length of time at heights around the 21,000-ft. mark in the hope of eventually getting acclimatized. Under atmospheric conditions similar to those prevailing at that altitude it was found that animal life could not continue for long. Although results may differ as between animals and human beings, there is no doubt that a marked decline in vitality sets in at such heights.

Hingston compares the dual mutually-conflicting physical pro-

cesses—acclimatization on the one hand and deterioration on the other—with what occurs in the case of the habitual drunkard. Excessive drinking leads to gradual bodily degeneration. At the same time the drunkard's body is constantly trying to adapt itself to resist the effects of quantities of alcohol, quantities often large enough to prove fatal if taken by a teetotaller.

It is impossible, even after the most thorough medical examination, to predict with any certainty how this or that individual is going to react to conditions at great heights. Mountaineers, with splendid achievements to their credit in the Alps, have frequently been known to fail in the Himalayas purely because they lacked the capacity to get acclimatized. What is more, it appears that the body's capacity to attune itself to changed conditions does not remain constant in one and the same person.

Our Andes expedition was too modest to allow for the inclusion of a doctor, and throughout our stay in the Cordillera Blanca we had neither the time nor the inclination to keep any such systematic records as might well lie within the province of a layman. We think some of our personal reactions may be of general interest, however.

Mountain-sickness in the Andes—or 'Soroche', as it is called—is particularly notorious. Its prevalence has a direct connection with the easy accessibility of the Andes and with the rapid climb that it is possible to make from the plains on the coast to the high passes, which generally lie at altitudes above 13,000 feet. With modern transport this transition to great heights can, of course, be effected in a matter of hours. Shortly after our arrival in Perú we ourselves went up to the pass which crosses the Cordillera Negra. This pass was at the 13,000-ft. level, and I succumbed almost immediately to an acute attack of soroche, which began with a feeling of unsteadiness, almost akin to that of inebriation. This later developed into a splitting headache, which was accompanied by a complete incapacity to make the slightest exertion.

That mountain-sickness dare not be taken lightly was underlined

178

by what we heard during our stay. Along that selfsame pass through the Cordillera Negra, where I myself fell victim to the dread scourge, no less than three people died as a direct result of mountain-sickness within the space of four months.

Members of the Austro-German expedition were reported to have had no trouble with the soroche. It must be remembered, however, that at the time these mountaineers were making their way towards the Cordillera Blanca, no roads for motor transport existed; so the slow journey thither by mule ensured in itself their acquiring *en route* a high degree of acclimatization. The American expedition, operating in the Cordillera Blanca about the same time as ours, lost one of its members in tragic circumstances. They had gone fairly rapidly to a height of over 16,500 feet. During the first night at this high altitude one of the Americans lost consciousness as a result of soroche, and, though a doctor was available, he died two days later while being transported down.

But, to come back to our own experiences.

Once down from the high pass and arrived at Ticapampa, which was about 11,500 feet above sea-level, the acute symptoms of mountain-sickness suffered by De Booy and myself disappeared almost at once. The only trouble that persisted was a pronounced breathlessness which obliged us to take things as quietly as possible. This, however, was something we had expected. Before our departure to Perú all sorts of authorities had expressedly warned us that it was most inadvisable to attempt to force matters. We had already made up our minds therefore to 'go slow'.

After several days at the 11,500-ft. level our general condition so improved that we thought ourselves fit enough to get up into the mountains. We were under the impression that a climb of some 2,000 feet would not involve too drastic a transition. We established a geological base camp at 13,450 feet and during the next few days started research work between 13,000 and 14,500 feet. Even this relatively small change in altitude over Ticapampa proved too

much for our constitutions. For days we were in a sorry plight and in no fit condition to do any really effective fieldwork. The slightest exertion brought on breathlessness and our headaches were chronic. We felt so out of sorts that, when it became necessary to climb some forty feet or so to get at some interesting rock, we used to toss up to decide who should do it. At that time I had definitely given up hope of ever becoming sufficiently acclimatized to be able to attempt the summit of the Huantsán, rising as it did to nearly 21,000 feet. The only small consolation was that both of us were experiencing the same sort of symptoms.

After a few days at 13,450 feet an appreciable improvement became noticeable and we bucked up considerably as our bodies began to get attuned. In fact, our condition bettered so rapidly that on the fifth day in the mountains we succeeded in climbing a peak reaching up to 16,000 feet: a record for both of us. And the more acclimatized we became, so also did the severity of the headaches diminish. When we returned to Ticapampa about three weeks later, it was as though we were back at sea-level. We bounded upstairs and carried on just as if we were at home. Eventually, a day's fieldwork on the mountains did not bother us at all, even at the 16,500-ft. level.

As our accounts of the climbs in the Pongos massif reveal, De Booy and I—after a month's acclimatization—were able to climb a summit rising to nearly 18,000 feet without experiencing any undue hardship or breathing difficulties. And, after that, attuning went on *crescendo*. In another two weeks' time there we were, up at 18,000 feet, actually blowing up air-mattresses with our mouths, although we had brought special bellows for doing that. We were then in tip-top form, which was just as well, for our attack on our most ambitious objective, the Huantsán, lay immediately ahead.

The still higher altitudes then reached had, of course, their usual adverse effect on our climbing performance. Below the 16,500-ft. level—in the so-called 'intermediate terrain'—De Booy and I were

The Nevado Pucaranra (20,167 feet)

able to maintain the regular Alpinist's climbing rate of about 1,300 feet per hour. But once over that mark, previous training and acclimatization notwithstanding, our pace became slower and we often stopped after a difficult passage, panting for breath. Breathlessness is, of course, materially influenced by one's physical condition at any given moment—as was my personal experience during the Huantsán ascent. The long, but comparatively simple trip on the third day from Camp 3 at 19,350 feet, over the 20,056-ft. north summit, to Camp 4 at 19,850 feet—following the previous day's exhausting efforts—was for me a veritable martyrdom. The fourth day, on the other hand, saw me making the far more complicated climb up to the south summit at 20,981 feet without any undue breathing handicap.

There is no doubt that personal idiosyncrasies play an important part in the attuning process. For instance, though the acclimatization of De Booy and myself took a completely parallel course at first, it became evident, once we were above 16,500 feet, that his 'top-altitude' or ceiling was higher than mine, proving that, quite apart from differences in age and weight, other individual factors entered into it.

Another thing that came to light during our stay in the Cordillera Blanca was my own extreme sensitivity to comparatively small changes in altitude. Whenever we went from Ticapampa up to our base camp, a journey involving a change of altitude of about 2,000 feet, I would always get, that same evening, a slight headache which, however, happily disappeared next day. This susceptibility of mine was not confined solely to ascents; a descent of 3,000 feet or so would also nearly always bring on a slight headache. This was never the case with De Booy.

Terray seemed far more immune to the throes of acclimatization than we Lowlanders. Within five days of his arrival at Lima—at sea-level—he was ready to undertake the climbing of the Pongos,

Base camp used for geological work in the Quilcahuanca valley

which was by no means an easy ascent, but one which he neverthe-less headed in dashing style. It was typical that, at the 18,737-ft. summit of this mountain, his only trouble was a little headache. It is difficult to say how much this imperviousness to height resulted from his climbing to over 23,000 feet three months earlier during the Aconcagua ascent.

Sleeplessness is also one of the ill effects of the lack of oxygen. All three of us suffered from this—the 'cast-iron' Terray perhaps most of all—and in the camps over 16,500 feet this wretched insomnia was often very troublesome. Again and again we had to have re-course to narcotics; and the higher we went the larger the dose needed. A strange peculiarity of our type of sleeplessness was that we did not get the low, jaded feeling normally experienced after a night of insomnia. Time after time, after a most miserable sleep-less night I got up feeling surprisingly fresh, able to face the heavy tasks ahead without undue qualms. Our sleeplessness was never attributable to the severe cold. The special down sleeping-bags gave us ample protection, even against the bitter temperatures experienced at the 20,000-ft. level.

Another effect of great height is loss of appetite. Above 16,500 feet it proved impossible to consume sufficient food to keep up weight, and we found anything containing the least trace of fat positively revolting. During the climbs we lived to a great extent on our bodily reserves, which fortunately stood up to the severe strain.

We did not experience in the Cordillera Blanca any of the mental disturbances which are commonly reputed to occur at high alti-tudes. We were, of course, not so very high compared with the Himalayas, but even at our heights mental disorders have been know to occur, as Terray could confirm having first-hand know-ledge of this sort of thing. Several months earlier, he had pressed forward with his climb of the Aconcagua without allowing suffi-cient time for proper acclimatization, and during the last section of the ascent he could not for the life of him remember who his com-

panion was, though it happened to be an Argentinian officer with whom for weeks on end he had been rubbing shoulders.

That little mental aberration of Terray was not so odd as that suffered by another climber on the Aconcagua. He is said to have suddenly remarked to his companion: 'Oh, I'm *so* sleepy! But it does not matter for I've just come across a library. I'm going in to have a doze in a book.' Whereupon he calmly stretched out his limbs on a flat slab.

It is undoubtedly difficult to retain one's powers of concentration at great heights. One member of a Himalayan expedition had so much trouble in this respect at 16,500 feet that eight acclimatizing days went by before he could concentrate sufficiently to write his first article for the press.

Such phenomena did not occur in our case thanks, of course, to our more gradual and effective period of acclimatization. As described in the account of the blizzard, a draft scheme for this book was actually drawn up whilst we were marooned at 18,000 feet.

In the Himalayas lack of oxygen above 26,000 feet becomes so acute that recourse has to be made to oxygen cylinders. The scaling of the 29,000-ft. summit of Mount Everest would never have been possible without this expedient. The comparatively low summits in the Andes can, however, be climbed by any normal, fit person without the aid of oxygen apparatus.

The inhabitants of the high plateaux of Perú, who spend the whole of their lives at heights of 10,000 feet or over, naturally have an advantage over us Europeans. One glance at these mountain-Indians, with their abnormally broad and deep chests, is enough to show that we cannot possibly hope to measure ourselves against them, though—according to Terray—they compare unfavourably with the famous Sherpas in the Himalayas as regards physical endurance and capacity to face danger and privation. But time and time again we were staggered at the ease with which Guillermo and

183

Pelegrino shouldered burdens of up to 110 lb. and at altitudes around 16,500 feet, too. It was strange though that both our porters had a touch of mountain-sickness when we reached 17,000 feet during the Pongos climb. They also required, apparently, a period of acclimatization on going up to a higher altitude.

That an acquired degree of acclimatization can be speedily lost was brought home to us when later we flew from Lima to Cuzco and return. We made the outward passage one week after our stay in the Cordillera Blanca, flying in an aeroplane which had no pressurized cabin. At an altitude of 19,500 feet passengers were given oxygen tubes to put in their mouths. At that time De Booy and I were so well attuned to that height that we had no need of oxygen, much to the surprise of our fellow-passengers. But when, after a five weeks' sojourn below the 6,500-ft. level, I returned to Lima, I was only too glad to avail myself of this artificial source of oxygen.

The difference between 'Andinism' and Alpinism, as practised in Europe is, of course, not purely one of acclimatization. In the mighty mountain world of the Andes one is completely isolated and has necessarily to be self-supporting. At eventide no comfortable mountain-hut conveniently awaits the climber after an exhausting day's work in the Cordillera Blanca. He has invariably to make his own camp in that wilderness of snow and ice, by pitching his tent somewhere on a glacier or on some level place up a ridge.

As soon as the technical difficulties get beyond the capabilities of porters, the climber is forced to do everything himself. At the end of a trying day he is confronted with the necessity of cooking a warm meal, a major operation in itself, for the low barometric pressure makes the melting of snow at 16,000 feet a long-drawn-out business. A hot meal is of vital importance, however, in building up one's resistance to the effects of the privations experienced at great heights.

Finally, there are the heavy loads that the climber himself has to

carry. In the Alps it is rare for one to have to shoulder a load of (say) 44 lb. other than up a simple mountain route on the way to a hut. During the climbing of the Huantsán there was no way of dodging having to lug along loads much above 44 lb. Moreover it was over terrain which was anything but simple. Negotiating an ice-slope with a gradient of 50 degrees is no child's play at the best of times, let alone with a heavy cumbersome rucksack tugging at one's back. In order to see the Huantsán attack through, we had to take with us sleeping-bags, a three-man tent, spare clothing, provisions for a full week on the mountain, cooking apparatus and fuel, photographic material, together with other indispensables such as a good supply of pitons, a spare 200-ft. rope, and other necessities of that kind.

Another great difference is that the day is much shorter there than in the Alps. During the climbing season in the Cordillera Blanca the sun does not rise until six o'clock. In the evening it disappears again at six, and as there is hardly any twilight in the tropics it is pitch dark by half-past six. The climber has thus only twelve hours of daylight, and he often cannot use these fully, for it can be so freezingly cold in the early morning at great heights that to venture out of the tent before the sun starts really giving out some warmth is simply to ask for frost-bite.

The technical climbing problems facing the mountaineer in the Cordillera Blanca are also quite different in certain respects from those encountered in European ranges. The enormous cornices which in most cases fringe the ridges, make these natural routes up the mountain both difficult and dangerous. Woe to the climber who underestimates the hazardous perils of those overhanging masses of snow and ice! Sometimes we found it possible to avoid them by making wide detours. Sometimes such deviations were definitely not possible—and then came the most unnerving moments of our climbs.

Mountaineering in the 'White Chain' consists for the most part in climbing on snow and ice. Where, as on the Pongos, the ridges

are broken by protruding rock buttresses, these are mostly so sheathed with ice that it is best to avoid them.

But it is not the massive cornice nor the ice-plastered rock, but rather the other factors previously mentioned which confront the climber in the Cordillera Blanca with such totally different problems from those met in the Alps. For us, the Pongos was technically perhaps the most difficult to tackle, the complications being, however, essentially of a climbing nature.

With the Huantsán it was different. This mountain had unique qualities, a challenge, unlike anything met in the Alps. In addition to the trials which any climb at very high altitude entails, we were hard put to it by reason of the excessive length of the climb. The ridge up which we had to toil was nearly two miles in length. Taken individually the difficulties on the *arête* were seldom exceptionally severe. But there were so *many* of them cropping up continually all along most part of it.

The Huantsán was—as mountains go—something completely new for De Booy and me. Terray felt this, too. He later acknowledged that he regarded its ascent as one of the supreme achievements of his whole career, particularly when he recalled that it was not accomplished by a full-sized, well-supported expedition, but by a small team of three—three who, for a period of six days, were thrown entirely on their own resources without the remotest chance of securing any outside help or succour.

But still, is it not precisely this last, with all its inherent risks, which gives an enterprise like ours such a singular charm?

SOMETHING
ABOUT GEOLOGY

In this chapter it is proposed to deal—very briefly, of course—with some geological aspects of the Cordillera Blanca in Perú.

At the outset it would perhaps be as well to explain why our choice fell on the Cordillera Blanca, what scientific reasons led to its selection as the objective of our expedition, and why our activities were concentrated in the southern part of the range.

Except in those places where drill-holes or mine-galleries afford some insight into rock structure below the earth's surface, geological interpretation is greatly hampered by the paucity of data on the course of geological structure in a vertical sense. In fact, in most places this course has largely to be inferred, to the best of the geologist's ability, from data available at the earth's surface—data which often leave ample room for uncertainty. From a research point of view it is fortunate that such places are to be found as the walls of fjords, or, better still, the deeply-eroded parts of high mountain ranges, where it is possible for the geologist, if a mountaineer, to collect data on geological structures in a vertical sense over well-exposed areas covering thousands of square yards.

Following the decision to make the South-American Andes our objective, study of relevant literature—including, of course, Steinmann's classic work *Geologie von Perú*[1]—quickly focused our at-

[1] *Geologie von Perú* by G. Steinmann, Heidelberg, 1929.

187

tention on the Cordillera Blanca, a range consisting largely of granodiorite (a rock-type closely related to granite), exposed by erosion.

In geological circles the origin of granite and related rocks is a topic of special current interest. The views of the 'Magmatists' who consider that these rock-types were formed in the earth's crust by the crystallization of a more or less fluid magma (comparable to the solidification on the earth's surface of lava from a volcano) are contrary to those held by the so-called 'Transformists' who consider that they were formed *in situ* by the transformation of pre-existing rock—a view which has lately gained considerable support. Others, taking less extreme points of view, deem both modes of origin to be possible. The well-known English petrologist, Read, has probably summed up the situation correctly with his remark that 'there are granites and granites'.

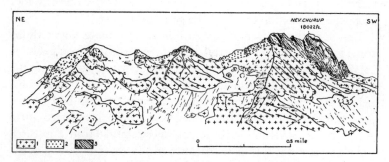

Sketch of Nevado Churup, as viewed from the N.
1. "White" granodiorite. 2. "Grey"-granodiorite. 3. Contact metamorphic sediments (lower neocomian slate-sandstone formation).

Having previously been occupied with problems of this particular nature elsewhere, the author came to the conclusion that the Cordillera Blanca was a most attractive region for investigation. There was also this advantage: the range was cut in many places by

Geology at great height

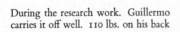

During the research work. Guillermo
carries it off well. 110 lbs. on his back

deep valleys (called *Quebradas* out there) running transverse to its general trend—a feature which would greatly facilitate the work of exploration.

* The decision to operate in the southern portion of the range was chiefly influenced by the fact that there the granodiorite bodies are relatively small and do not, as is the case in the northern part of the range, monopolize almost its whole breadth. The southern part would therefore permit of a more effective study of the relationships between the granodiorites and their adjacent rocks.

The aims we had in view were thus purely scientific and not, as many people erroneously assumed, dictated by economic considerations, such as prospecting for valuable ores. Perú is, of course, noted for its mineral potentialities. Had these been our objective we certainly should not have picked the Cordillera Blanca, but would have gone to one of the other ranges in the Peruvian Andes where mineral deposits are known to be present.

We were often asked what value such a purely scientific exploration could have and why it was necessary, in any case, to conduct it in the far-off Cordilleras of Perú. In reply we could only point out that it is often quite impossible to foretell to what extent a scientific research may ultimately prove, if only indirectly, of economic worth. Whether in fact any material benefit will eventually result from our mission is somewhat beside the point. But there is this much to be said. Painstaking exploration of any particular area, wherever it may be, is bound to lead to a better insight into the composition and structure of the earth's crust and thus forms in itself a contribution to general knowledge.

Although from a distance the Cordillera Blanca gives the impression of being wild and inaccessible, actually the central parts of the range can be reached fairly easily through the cross-cutting quebradas, which provide natural and quick means of approach by horse or mule. Furthermore, these quebradas frequently branch out

Glacier—calving off

at their higher reaches into smaller subsidiary valleys—an advantageous physical feature, leading to a considerable saving of time and energy, and sparing the geologist much arduous climbing of steep slopes at altitudes over 15,000 feet, where such manœuvring is always a slow and exhausting business. For this reason we worked valley after valley systematically and only crossed from one to another when absolutely necessary for our investigations.

In point of fact, our geological explorations resulted in our making ten distinct trips from our Ticapampa headquarters. One, or at the most two, of the main quebradas were visited each trip and the surrounding mountains investigated and mapped. On each occasion we started off with pack animals, equipment, and sufficient provisions for a stay of one or two weeks high up the range. We usually established base camp as far up the main quebrada as possible, preferably close to its junction with one or two smaller valleys or near some interesting geological formations. Once camp was pitched—mostly at heights between 13,000 and 15,000 feet—field-work began forthwith and trips were made daily. Whenever possible we returned to spend nights in base camp; but when research work took us high up the mountain-side or too far away, we used to pitch a small two-man tent and sleep somewhere at high altitude.

Reference has been made in a previous chapter to the enormous length of the *Cordilleras de los Andes*, that succession of mountain chains and plateaux extending all along the west side of the South American continent and stretching over more than 65 degrees of latitude. The Andes, like the Alps and the Himalayas, is a folded mountain chain—but with this important difference: the folding of the Andes was much less intense than that responsible for the formation of the Alps and Himalayas, where it gave rise to large-scale overthrusting, causing parts of the earth's crust to be displaced tens of miles in distance and highly complicated structures to be formed.

The structure of the Andes is, generally speaking, uncomplicated. That is certainly true of the Cordillera Blanca, where the sedimentary series reveal a fairly simple form of folding. No large-scale overthrusting of the Alpine type appears to have taken place. Where any evidence of thrusting does come to light, both the horizontal and the vertical displacements seem to have been relatively slight.

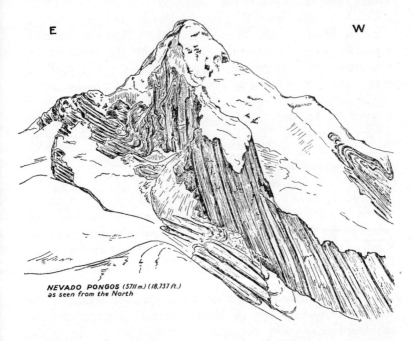

E   W

NEVADO PONGOS (5711 m.) (18,737 ft.)
as seen from the North

In many parts of the investigated region the folds were found to be almost symmetrical. Generally they showed a marked tendency to be overturned towards the east. A good example of this type of folding is illustrated above. This is a reproduction of one of the field sketches made during the course of the exploration. The drawing shows the Pongos, viewed from the north. One can

clearly see how the rocks forming the mountain (in this case—quartzites) are folded and, as it were, partially crumpled.

The folded sedimentary strata in the investigated region all belong to the Lower Cretaceous. They belong chiefly to the monotonous series of argillaceous and arenaceous rocks of mainly terrestrial origin—considered in the Peruvian Cordilleras to represent the Lower Neocomian part of the Cretaceous.

On the eastern side of the range coal-seams are found here and there in the series. The slate-sandstone formation also contains, especially along the western slopes, conglomeratic intercalations, sometimes with large pebbles. It is poor in fossils; in fact, fossilized plant remains were found only in the vicinity of the coal-seams.

The slate-sandstone formation on the eastern side of the range is covered by limestones, considered to represent the base of the Upper Neocomian. Then follows a thick series in which sandstones and marls predominate, whilst the succession is closed by fossiliferous limestones of marine origin.

Intensive volcanic activity apparently played an important role in the evolution of the Andes. Indeed, vulcanism is still active in many places in the Andes. In the Peruvian section it is confined to the south of the country. No volcanic activity has occurred in recent time in the Cordillera Blanca itself, but there is ample evidence of eruptions in earlier geological periods.

In the Lower Neocomian series, volcanic and sub-volcanic rocks were found to be widely distributed. In many instances they are developed as so-called sills, formed by injection parallel to the stratification of the sediments. Good examples of such concordant bodies were found on the eastern side of the range, i.e. in the slate-sandstone formation directly below the Yanashallash Pass (shewn on page 195). In other cases, sub-volcanic bodies were found to intersect the sediments. Sometimes they also gave the impression of having been formed at the earth's surface as lava-flows or by vol-

canic explosion (agglomerates and tuffs). Volcanics of this latter type are of such extensive distribution at two places in the investigated region as to warrant indication on the geological sketch map. One of these is the massif of the Nevado Huantsán, the more than 6,600-ft. high south-eastern face of which seems to consist of an uninterrupted succession of volcanic material.

Previously, all the high summits in the Cordillera Blanca were thought to consist of granodiorite. One might well ask why the highest mountains should invariably be found to be granodiorite or, in some cases, volcanic rocks. The reason is mainly that these rock types, owing to their structure and hardness, have proved far more resistant to erosion than the sediments surrounding them. Microscopic examination of samples of the volcanic and subvolcanic rocks revealed that most varieties contained a percentage of silica ranging from medium to high. They are chiefly andesites and dacites, but rhyolites are also present.

The Cretaceous in the Peruvian Andes was hitherto thought to contain only volcanics of a basic (Silica-poor) type. In the investigated region these were found to be of but subordinate importance. It is clearly impossible to determine in every case the relative age of these igneous rocks. A striking feature, however, was that the conglomeratic intercalations in the Lower Neocomian slate-sandstone formation were found to contain pebbles of dacitic and andesitic rocks, indicating that volcanic activity must have occurred prior to the deposition of these conglomerates, viz. during or prior to the Lower Neocomian. This is significant, as otherwise one might presume that the magmas (from which the aforementioned sills solidified) had been intruded at a later date. Whether the volcanics of the Huantsán might similarly be regarded as proper to the Lower Neocomian or whether, in fact, they are somewhat younger in origin has not yet been proved.

One cannot fix precisely when the mountain-building movements responsible for the folding in the Cordillera Blanca occurred,

as post-Neocomian sediments are mainly absent. A first orogenic phase is known to have taken place in other parts of the Peruvian Andes towards the end of the Cretaceous. The main phase, responsible also for the folding of the Cordillera Blanca, must have occurred in the Earlier Tertiary. A third phase of much less intensity seems to have taken place in the Pliocene.

In many places in the Andes, such as north Bolivia, south Perú, and the Cordillera Blanca, the main orogenic phase was followed by the formation of the granodioritic and related varieties of rocks. As previously mentioned, separate bodies of these plutonic rocks (mainly granodiorites and the closely related quartz-diorites) of considerable dimensions are to be found in the Cordillera Blanca. Separate masses, extending tens of miles across, occur in the northern part of the range, while the expeditionary area itself also contains fairly large granodioritic bodies, especially on the western side. To the extreme south these often appear to be fairly homogeneous in composition over considerable areas. In the north of the area, however, complications occur. Here it was possible to distinguish several bodies (not separately indicated on the map) by their composition and to ascertain their order of formation, i.e. in order of increasing acidity. The relationship between two of these rock bodies is illustrated in the sketch on page 188. The younger 'white' granodiorite occurring in this figure forms veins in the slightly more basic 'grey' granodiorite. These veins are too small, however, to be shewn in the sketch. The quartz-diorites are accompanied in some places by dike rocks of similar composition.

The formation of the plutonic rocks—which, in the Cordillera Blanca, are considered to have crystallized, at least for the greater part, out of magma, though some transformation of pre-existing rocks has undoubtedly also taken place—is deemed to have proceeded during the Lower to Middle Tertiary. Their emplacement, in any case, took place subsequent to the main phase of the folding. The various granodioritic masses are admittedly stretched in con-

Geological sketch map of part of the southern Cordillera Blanca

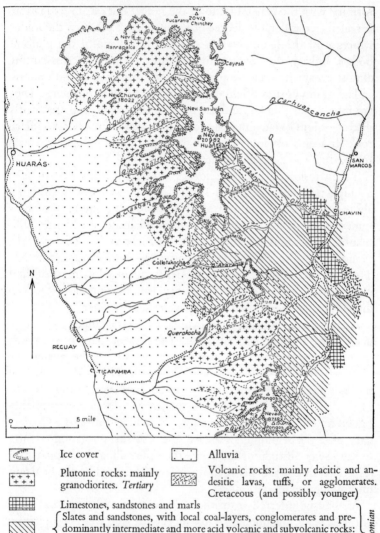

	Ice cover		Alluvia
+++	Plutonic rocks: mainly granodiorites. *Tertiary*		Volcanic rocks: mainly dacitic and andesitic lavas, tuffs, or agglomerates. Cretaceous (and possibly younger)

Limestones, sandstones and marls

{ Slates and sandstones, with local coal-layers, conglomerates and predominantly intermediate and more acid volcanic and subvolcanic rocks: "slate-sandstone formation"

Ditto, thermally metamorphic; mainly hornfelses and quartzites

Neocomian

formity with the general trend of the range; but our investigations revealed a considerable degree of independence between the folded structure of the sedimentary series and the shape of the plutonic bodies. Indeed, the contacts of the latter are clearly cross-cutting almost everywhere in the area—contrary to previous assumptions.

The granodiorites often afforded evidence of movements. They are intensively jointed; and microscopical examination frequently disclosed signs of late internal movements in the already crystallized rock. It seems obvious that the third and last folding phase was responsible for these phenomena.

The intrusion of the granodiorites and related rocks was attended by high temperatures which affected the adjacent rocks, bringing about re-crystallization and also frequently the creation of new minerals altogether, such as biotite, andalusite, cordierite, sillimanite, and garnet. In other words, the rocks in the vicinity of the granodiorites—in the so-called *contact zone*—were metamorphosed. The volcanics in the Cretaceous series frequently lost most of their initial structure during their metamorphism. In some cases it is even difficult to recognize their original volcanic character.

After the last orogenic phase denudation of the range increasingly became the main geological factor. The present shape of the range over the 13,000-ft. level is mainly attributable to the quaternary glaciation, itself divisible into several periods. The final contours of the mountain range were mainly carved, however, during the last of the glaciations. According to Steinmann, this was presumably caused by the elevation of the range as a whole during the Quaternary, after the beginning of the Ice Age. The first glaciations, owing to the lower altitude of the range then prevailing, had apparently less effect, their traces being more or less obliterated by the final and most extensive glaciation.

As may be inferred from their characteristic U-shape and their polished walls, the quebradas during the Ice Age were occupied by immense glaciers. As a result of post-glacial changes in climate,

however, the glaciers have gradually receded more and more to higher regions. According to Steinmann, the snow-line during the last pleistocene glaciation was 2,000–2,300 feet lower than it is at present. In the White Cordillera the line nowadays occurs round the 16,000-ft. mark (as compared with approximately 10,000-ft. mark in the Alps). The numerous glaciers still descending from the central parts of the range seldom reach a level lower than 14,000 feet. The main quebradas are usually, therefore, free from ice.

The snow-line is still retreating upwards in the Andes, as is the case almost everywhere else on the globe. Heim[1] estimates that it has risen 150 to 200 metres (500–650 feet) since 1850. After the Ice Age the glaciers succeeded at first in maintaining an existence high up in the quebradas—a fact demonstrated by the exceptionally fine end-moraines found in the higher reaches of the valleys. But recent changes in glaciation have given rise to a phenomenon which has manifested itself on several occasions in the investigated part of the Cordillera Blanca and in a tragic manner.

Renewed regression has caused the glacier tongues (or lower ends) once more to withdraw upwards so that there is now a tendency for huge volumes of melt-water to collect between the receding tongues and the end-moraines, the latter often functioning, temporarily at any rate, as natural dams. In this way lakes, or *lagunas* as they are called in Perú, are formed. On the western side of the range lakes of this type sometimes extend over a mile in length.

It would be most unwise to underestimate the dangers inherent in these *lagunas*, imperilling as they do not only the mountain regions but also the more thickly populated valleys on both sides of the range—the Santa valley, and the valley of the Mosna. The threat arises in every case where the end-moraine does not allow of adequate off-drainage. Without a steady and sufficient flow away, the water level in the lake naturally rises higher and higher, constantly

[1] Arn. Heim on the 'Glaciation of South America, as related to Tectonics-Observations, 1939–1947'. Ecl. Geol. Helv. 44-1-1951.

increasing the pressure on the moraine-dam. The latter is actually only a rampart of loose blocks and debris of all sorts. The dam has, therefore, little real compactness and not much is needed to force a break. In some cases the increasing water pressure may be sufficient in itself to cause a collapse. In other instances a break-through may be caused when large masses of ice 'calve-off' from a glacier and fall into a lake. The wash occasioned by an immense block of ice crashing down into the water may send a mighty wave surging over the moraine-dam, which is then all too apt to give way. The lake empties itself through the breach in the dam. The water, sweeping downwards with part of the moraine, hurls itself through the valley, uprooting everything that can be torn loose and borne in transit. It sometimes comes cascading down as far as the principal broad valley running parallel to the range.

A catastrophic instance of an *aluvión* of this type occurred in January 1941 when a *laguna*-dam collapsed at the upper end of the Cohup valley (north of our expeditionary area). A flood of mud and boulders rushed six miles or so down the quebrada and finally swooped into the Santa valley. The small town of Huaraz was partly submerged, a third of the place was entirely devastated, and more than 5,000 people were buried alive.

During our stay in the Cordillera Blanca we had occasion once or twice to follow the path of this dreadful debris-stream upwards from Huaraz. Time and again we stood amazed at the almost incredible amount of material brought down at the time of the disaster. Huge blocks, some over 20 feet in diameter, were strewn haphazardly along the route. At various places sad crosses indicated where entire families had perished.

Huaraz was not the only place to suffer in this way. In 1945 a similar fate overtook the village of Chavin on the east side of the range. In this case the debris-stream is said to have caused the deaths of some 500 people.

This danger still threatens from several quarters. The Peruvian

authorities are fully alive, however, to the necessity of taking pre-
ventive measures to avoid further catastrophes of this type. A
special commission, aided by foreign experts, is charged with the
task of keeping unremitting watch on water levels at critical points.
Steps are taken, when necessary and wherever practicable, to drain
off water artificially, so as to keep the level and the pressure in the
glacial lagoons within safe limits.

Our scientific programme in the Cordillera Blanca was completed according to plan. Our field-work included an intensive
study of the granodiorites and related rocks, and—in direct connection with these—of the metamorphism of the country rock. Some
insight was also gained into the relationships between the structure
and shape of the plutonic bodies, which are considered to be, for the
main part, of an intrusive nature. We furthermore prepared a
geological map of terrain covering roughly 1,000 square kilometres
(approximately 600 square miles), most of it above the 13,000-ft.
level. Exploratory work at high altitude led in several instances to
very satisfactory results. It stands to reason, however, that solutions
have not been found to each and every problem. Nevertheless an
advance, modest though it may be, in our general knowledge of the
Andes has undoubtedly resulted from these investigations.

ACKNOWLEDGMENTS

The Dutch expedition to the Peruvian Andes was in the field from May to September 1952 and the major portion of this time was devoted to geological research work in the southern part of the Cordillera Blanca. These scientific investigations were indeed the primary purpose of our mission to Perú. Only a period of about five weeks could be allotted in which to attempt a number of first ascents.

Nevertheless it is this comparatively brief climbing portion of our stay and what happened on our ascents of the Queshque and the Pongos, on our conquest—after two defeats—of the mighty Huantsán, which are described in this book. Much of the material was conceived—some of it actually written—whilst Terray, De Booy and I were still up there in that far-off white Andes world of snow and ice, aloof and isolated from human contact. Thus it is that the story unavoidably revolves round and concentrates on just the three of us.

None of the things which occurred to us could possibly have taken place, however, without the co-operation and help of many, many others. My two fellow expedition members and I cannot end this book without paying tribute to these good friends. We are only sorry that there is insufficient space to permit of detailed acknowledgments. But to all who assisted us in any way—whether mentioned or not—we here and now place on record our deep and sincere gratitude.

The Hon. C. J. A. Ranitz, the President of the Royal Nether-

lands Alpine Club has written[1] of his reactions on 13th July 1952 when, seated in a wicker chair, enjoying the morning sun in the garden of a country house in Twente, his eye fell on a brief report in a Dutch newspaper of our victory over Huantsán. It was a thrilling, unforgettable moment, he said, and all that day he had been quite beside himself, flushed with pride and joy at our success. To his mind flashed memories of earlier Dutch explorers and navigators, Tasman, Linschoten, Houtman, Heemskerk, Barentz—to mention but a few whose names are now indelibly written on the map of the world. On the mountaineering side he paid us the compliment of adding our names to the list of Dutch climbers who in the past have brought off so many fine achievements. He recalled Sillem, the first Netherlander to climb the Matterhorn, the Visser-Hoofts—husband and wife—who made four expeditions to the Himalayas and Karakoram, and the equally intrepid pioneering work of climbers like Lorentz, Nouhuys, Herderschee, Colijn, Dozy and Wissel in New Guinea.

We in turn would here like to pay *our* tribute to him not only as a fine mountaineer himself and not only in his guiding capacity as President of the Royal Netherlands Alpine Club, which sponsored our mission, but also as the inspirer who was 'with us' from the very first and backed us to the very last.

The other members of the Club's Executive Committee were splendid, too; and we became deeply indebted to the honorary member, Dr. P. C. Visser, whose name is so closely linked with Dutch mountaineering and who perhaps has done more than any other individual to raise the Netherlands' prestige in this field outside Europe.

Foreign climbing circles showed considerable interest in our plans. René Mailleux, for instance, the vice-President of the Belgian Alpine Club, gave us the benefit of his experiences during

[1] The Hon. C. J. A. Ranitz wrote a glowing Foreword to the original Dutch edition: *Naar onbes-tegen Andes-toppen*:

the Franco-Belgian expedition of 1951 to the Cordillera Blanca. The French Himalayan Committee and the French Patagonian expedition generously loaned us equipment. The latter organization additionally put provisions at our disposal.

In non-climbing circles, too, there were many at home and abroad who helped us by word and deed. Among the personalities which spring to mind are Señor Enrique Goytisolo B., the then Peruvian Ambassador to the Hague, who took a keen interest in our plans from the start, gave us excellent advice on many aspects, and extended a helping hand generally; Dr. J. Kwast in Holland who so readily responded to our appeal for help in the medical field; and Professor Dr. H. A. Brouwer, Director of the Geological Institute of Amsterdam University, whose interest was, of course, primarily in the scientific side of our mission.

Whilst the expedition was operating in South America the co-operation and help given us by various Peruvian societies and bodies were especially heartening. We shall always think affectionately of our reception by members of the *Grupo Andinista Cordillera Blanca* at Huaraz; and we especially cherish the memory of the gracious hospitality we enjoyed at the house of Mr. and Mrs. Morales, the parents of our stalwart friend, Cesar, secretary of the Andinist Club.

We became indebted too, to Dr. H. J. Spann, a geographer, whose intimate knowledge of the Cordillera Blanca enabled him to give us any amount of invaluable advice. The fine aerial photograph of the Huantsán included in this book came from Dr. Spann's collection.

Financially we were indebted for contributions given in a most altruistic way not only by our sponsors, the Royal Netherlands Alpine Club, but other Dutch organizations such as the Netherlands Organization for Pure Research, the Royal Netherlands Geographical Society, the Royal Netherlands Geological and Mining

Society, the Prince Bernhard and Molengraaf Funds, Royal Dutch Airlines (K.L.M.) and the Royal Netherlands Steamship Company (K.V.S.M.). We wish to express our thanks, too, to the many concerns who let us have all sorts of stores either gratis or at greatly reduced prices; and who, therefore, like the rest, contributed in no small measure to our success.

We acknowledge thankfully the welcome and the assistance afforded us on various occasions by the Dutch Ambassador at Lima, His Excellency L. A. Gastmann, and at a later stage by his successor Ch. J. H. Daubanton. In addition to Legation assistance, we received welcome aid in an hour of need from another Dutchman, J. Corver, chief official of the Royal Netherlands Steamship Company in Perú. Thanks to his energetic help we were able to move off to the Cordillera Blanca and get down to work within a few days of our reaching Lima. Only those with experience of travelling the world with loads of gear and equipment can appreciate how easy it is to get bogged down and delayed by endless formalities.

During our stay in Perú powerful support for our cause at home was forthcoming in unstinted measure from our faithful ally, S. B. Spijer. He proved himself invaluable in looking after our interests generally, polishing up our articles for the press, developing our photographic material and making provisional classifications of rock samples. His activities in Holland helped in no small way to maintain the spirit and confidence of the team out there in Perú.

Then last—but definitely by no means least—we mention Mr. Kroupnitzky, the Manager of the Anglo-French Silver Mining Company, and his charming wife. We shall never forget their warm spontaneous welcome, nor the way in which they kept open house for us. It is good to know that such people as these are still to be found in odd, isolated places in this world, upholding the best traditions of European civilization. As Lionel Terray, on his own arrival at the Kroupnitzky home, put it: 'Nous sommes bien tombés ici!' Yes, we were indeed made to feel at home.